Nostalgia Home Plans

100 Time-Honored Designs Updated with Today's Features

Edited by Design Basics, Inc.
Published by Home Planners, LLC

Over the years, we at Design Basics have been bringing people home with many of America's most popular home plans. Our company began as a custom home plan design firm for the professional builders of our local community, Omaha, NE. As the popularity of our designs increased, we expanded our focus from designing for the local market only, to designing plans that would be adaptable anywhere. Since then, builder as well as consumer interest in our plans has grown tremendously in all 50 states and countries around the world.

Today we are one of the nation's largest home plan design companies, nationally recognized through numerous awards in design, business management, corporate growth and the development of effective marketing products. We offer a variety of home plans as well as products and services which include color renderings, estimator's material lists, plan changes and more.

Whether it's a product, service or one of our home plans, we take pride in serving you with our very best.

Nostalgia Home Plans

Editors	Kevin Blair
	Tina Leyden
Writer	Joyce Brown
Rendering Illustrators	Shawn Doherty
	Silvia Boyd
	Perry Gauthier
	George McDonald, dec.
Technical Advisor	Rob Phillips
Circulation Manager	Priscilla Ivey
Chief Executive Officer	Dennis Brozak
President	Linda Reimer
Director of Marketing	Kevin Blair
Business Development	Paul Foresman
Controller	Janie Murnane
Editor-in-Chief	Bruce Arant

Design, Text and Illustrations © 2000 by Design Basics, Inc.
Overall Publication © 2000 by Home Planners, LLC
All rights reserved.

Front Cover   Plan HPT040096, The Newberry
Built by Jarco Development
See pages 206-207

Back Cover   Plan HPT040028, The Marcell
Photo by © Phil Bell
Built by Dan Lowe Construction
See pages 70-71

design basics inc®
HOME PLAN DESIGN SERVICE

First Printing, September, 2000
1 0 9 8 7 6 5 4 3 2 1
Printed in the United States of America
Library of Congress Control Number: 00-026093
ISBN (softcover): 1-881955-69-9

Table of Contents

1-Story Homes

1¹/₂-Story Homes

2-Story Homes

The home in these photographs may be altered from the original pl[...]

Built by Dan Lowe Construction. For more information about the Marcell, see pages 70-[...]

A NEW APPROACH TO TIME-HONORED DESIGN

What is it we find so deeply alluring about home[s] of the past? Whether its a boxy Craftsman with roof brackets and divided light windows or a Victorian adorne[d] with turrets and finials, most of us are naturally draw[n] to homes seasoned with age. Full of character, the[y] bring back memories of houses we grew up in and st[ir] sentimental longings for slower, simpler times. With style so appealing it neve[r] becomes outdated, they remind us of an age when skilled craftsmen took pride i[n] everything they built and simple details made an impact. They are homes that in [a] sudden wave of sentiment, will inevitably prompt us to lament, "They su[re] don't make 'em like they used to."

Turn the pages and go back in time. The Nostalgia Home Pla[n] Collection™ from Design Basics was created to help you rediscover th[e] homes of yesteryear – particularly homes built around the turn of the cen[] tury. We chose to focus on this time period because it was then that Amer[i] can architecture really came into its own. In the post Civil War er[a,] industrialization allowed us to utilize our abundant natural resources. Th[e]

Exterior and Interior Photos: Phil Bell

ABOVE: MASTER BEDROOM
In the master bedroom, the use of scrolling wrought iron dictates the romantic flair of the past along with the knotted drapery – an updated version of bygone tassels.

nation's economy boomed until it rivaled Europe's. As we grew in power and influence, we naturally became more independent and began creating our own architectural styles. Advanced manufacturing techniques made it possible to mass-produce finished windows, doors, brackets and decorative turnings – often more elaborate than previous handmade versions.

More than likely, the following designs will cause you to think of houses you've admired while driving through the older neighborhoods of your hometown or of ones you've seen on the pages of historical home magazines. You'll be drawn to the time-honored detailing of their exteriors– entablatures, batten board shutters, corner boards and balustrades. You'll appreciate the beckoning welcome of deep front porches and the distinctive styling of steep massed roofs, brackets, fascias and cornices.

You'll discover the same type of nostalgic "fingerprints" in the homes' interiors. Quaint alcoves, built-in display cabinets, master suite sitting rooms and plentiful storage areas provide charm and convenience. Thick trim, dropped soffits, cornices and columns contribute a sense of quality found in vintage homes. Sloped and tall ceilings add interest and provide a sense of openness.

It was our intention to create each of these designs to stand on their own merit. Therefore, as much as you'll admire each design in this collection, you'll discover that none of them represent authentic historical architecture. Rather, they borrow the cherished warmth and careful artistry of homes of the past to create some-

ABOVE: KITCHEN
Wood tones were typically finished in oak, but the Marcell's updated kitchen uses a darker wood which still emits a warm nostalgic feeling.

BELOW: GREAT ROOM
The great room's vintage wall color was lighted for an updated look. The floral upholstery on the sofas and chairs was modernized with lighter colors and a less decorative pattern.

thing altogether unique.

The inherent beauty of these homes makes them fit in any neighborhood, yet stand out from others around them. Every design on the following pages provides the distinction of a one-of-a-kind home that up-coming generations will likewise admire and hope to live in.

Built by: GS Fedewa Builders

A variety of room arrangements have been included to suit today's varied lifestyles. And with nearly 30 plans under 1,850 square feet, there's something for every budget.

Our own definition of home went into designing the 100 homes in this collection. We've included 1-story, 1½-story and 2-story plans. They range in size from 1,191 to 3,480 square feet and reflect a wide variety of lifestyles and tastes. Yet with all of the rich diversity represented, they have one thing in common. Each embodies the spirit of what home is at its best – a place that brings families together again and again and brings an aching knot in their throats when it's time to leave. After all, that's our mission at Design Basics, where our purpose is: "Bringing People Home."

Classic features on the Patagonia's exterior (below) include tall, narrow, double-hung windows with mutton bar detailing; patterned brick; traditional shutters; double gables and dormers. To maintain a traditional look, the garage is camouflaged.

Built by: Mongold Construction, Inc.

The Calabretta (above) is a strong Colonial with shoulder coursing trim over double hung windows, traditional shutters and a gabled extension. A paneled door is surrounded by windows – a practical feature from the past to light entries.

The Nostalgic *touch*
INSIDE and OUT

While any decorating style will complement the homes in this collection, you may want to incorporate ideas and accessories from the past. Over the next few pages, we've provided a historical perspective, from interior to exterior, on many features that characterized homes from the turn of the century.

"Marble slab mantels graced fireplaces . . ."

Interiors

At the turn of the century, ceilings were high and rooms were dimly lit. Paneled wainscots, false beamed ceilings and parquet floors characterized the interiors of all "important" rooms. Walls were covered with wallpaper, painted stencil patterns and imitation Spanish leather to create a feeling of wealth.

Today's interiors offer tall ceilings but forgo the dimly-lit rooms by providing a variety of natural light sources. The use of richer wall colors still emits the warmth of a dimly lit room. Simple wood floors have replaced parquet. Historic wall treatments are still popular, but are often reproduced in faux finishes to reduce cost.

Woodwork

Interior trim included paneled wainscoting, beamed ceilings, heavy wood trim and massive moldings, usually finished in darker tones. Today, those elements have been scaled down in proportion to a home's styling and size. Moldings and wainscoting are painted or updated with lighter tones of wood.

Windows

were covered with heavy draperies, swags, valances and jabots, enriched with tassels and heavy fringes. Today's windows are drastically simplified, often decorated with a swag or sheer treatment over pleated shades or blinds. The tassels and heavy fringes of the past are being reintroduced in more delicate and subdued versions.

Fireplaces

Marble slab mantels graced fireplaces which often had ornamental arched openings. A luxury item today, marble can still add to an old-world feel of a home through the substitution of a painted faux finish.

Photos by: Gary Yasaka

"Room arrangements were pulled away from walls to create conversational groupings…"

Photos by: Gary Yasaka

"Walls were covered with wallpaper, painted stencil patterns and imitation Spanish leather to emit a feeling of wealth."

Kitchens

The common use of golden oak i kitchens and other cabinetry was a sign of respectability i a home, emitting a sense of richness to a room. Oak is still widely used in kitchens today. To provide time-worn feel, woodwork is also distressed or finished with washed paint.

Closets

One of the more curious aspects of homes from the turn of the century is the rarity o closets. With the frequent changing of clothes for day and evening wear, it seems strange that closets wer not in more abundance. The real explanation for the scarcity of closets was the abundance of servant Armoires solved immediate needs while maids retrieved clothes from an upstairs room (or attic) wher clothing was packed in chests. Large walk-in closets now replace the upstairs room. Armoires are ofte included among bedroom furnishings to bring back a sense of the past and for TV viewing.

Nostalgic UPHOLSTERY patterns

damask   tapestry   repetitive geometric   rich velvets
                                              pattern

"Popular fabrics of the time were often mismatched, such as damask, tapestry, repetitive geometric and rich velvets."

"Furniture of the early part of the century included legs with a turned treatment."

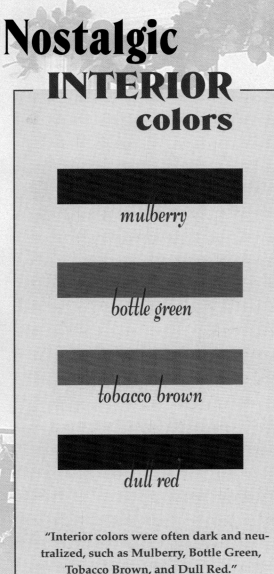

Nostalgic INTERIOR colors

mulberry

bottle green

tobacco brown

dull red

"Interior colors were often dark and neutralized, such as Mulberry, Bottle Green, Tobacco Brown, and Dull Red."

Furniture

In the early 1900's room arrangements were, for the first time, pulled away from the walls to create informal conversational gatherings. In keeping with the eclectic styling of the time, furniture pieces were not likely to be a matched set. Furniture was often upholstered in unmatched damask fabrics with elaborate cord, fringe, button and tassel trims.

With the relatively open design of today's room arrangements, "floating" furniture to create conversation areas is popular once again. Upholstery is more subdued in lighter colors and less ornate patterns.

Accessories

Seventy or eighty years ago the "lady of the house" brought beauty and sophistication to her home by combining all of the popular accessories of the time – easels, urns, pedestals and fans. The contemporary rendition of this styling accessorizes in simpler terms, selecting two or three complementing pieces to achieve the clean appearance favored today.

Colors

Interior colors were often dark and neutralized, such as Mulberry, Bottle Green, Tobacco Brown, and Dull Red. They were colors with muddy, time-worn hues that diffuse an essence of affluence. These same colors applied today are toned-down and lightened to coincide with simplified interiors.

Collections

America's fetish for collecting was in full swing during this era. Collections often adorned the halls and display cases within homes from this time. A common practice among Victorians was to label

Exterior photo and interior renderings are from The Gerard, featured on pages 192-193

each piece within carefully categorized collections. For the homes in this volume, displaying antiques or collectibles in the various built-in niches is a great way to add a timeless focal point to an entry, stairway or living area.

Exteriors
Steep gabled roofs, corner towers, balconies, dormers, scalloped shingles and brick detailing applied in patterns were common at the time. Classical elements such as cupolas, porte cocheres and bay windows were often oversized.

Today, costs and tastes require a simpler version. Builders and designers now use more of a toned-down approach with window trim, decorative ironwork and copper roofs. If columns, bays and cupolas are included, they are more accurately proportioned. Simple elements such as half-round gutters and round downspouts can add an old-fashioned touch.

Since few homes had attached garages at the time, many of the homes in this volume employ a side-load garage or special elements to incorporate the garage into the design.

Porches were prevalent in the era and offered the chance to socialize. Victorians popularized the sleeping porch to enjoy the rigors of the fresh night air. Today, porches have become extensions of living areas used for entertaining or private relaxation.

Landscaping
The homes of yesterday contributed to picturesque neighborhoods and streets. One way to bring a sense of the period to your home is through a walkway paved in brick or cobblestone. Incorporating a street lamp or wrought-iron bench into the landscaping can also add a nostalgic effect. Other garden-style touches such as sundials, vine-covered arbors or free-standing gazebos can further enhance the old-world feel.

Lawns
Cast iron figurines and gazing balls on pedestals were frequently included in the lawn ornamentation of the day. Roses, hydrangeas, larkspur and ferns were very popular. Herb gardens were also common. Today's landscaping offers homeowners a wider variety of vegetation. Planting varieties that are indigenous to the area can help give an "established" look to a yard.

yesterday's Home Today

We hope we've helped you visualize some ways to draw out the natural warmth and character from the designs in this collection. With the home that best suits your lifestyle, and a little foresight and planning, you will enjoy the best of yesterday and today.

ABOVE: MASTER BEDROOM
The master bedroom features corner windows that accent the room with a touch of light. A boxed ceiling enhances the overall spaciousness of the room.

ABOVE: KITCHEN
A view into the lovely kitchen reveals an efficient work area with island counter between the sink and stove.

BELOW: FAMILY ROOM
A cozy furniture grouping creates a natural conversation area around the fireplace in the family room. A set of triple-wide windows views the back and offers an abundance of light inside.

In the
Nostalgia *Collection you will find...*

SIMPLER FOUNDATIONS

While buyers will appreciate the old-world feel of these homes, they will also appreciate the lengths we went to throughout the design process to save them money on the construction of the home. For example, any protrusion or 'jog' in the foundation costs money. The simpler the foundation, the less costly it becomes. As much as we could, we tried to limit any protrusions in the foundation to the front of the home, to focus the most dramatic effects there. Conversely, we often squared off the foundations in the back for cost effectiveness.

DORMERS

Many of the designs in this collection feature front-to-back gables paired with dormers. This is a timeless elevation style that will be admired long into the future. Dormers tend to break up the monotony of the roofline and also create much of the charm on the front elevation. The addition of dormers also creates exciting alcoves in the second level rooms that can be used as cozy play areas for children or bright study spaces.

1-Story Homes

THE OAKFIELD

❶ A combined use of exterior materials, such as brick, stucco and copper accents, give this economical one-story its distinction.

❷ A stairway located in the garage leads to potential unfinished storage space.

❸ Boxed windows with deep sills offer elegant light sources for the great room and bedroom 3.

❹ An angled entry gives distinction to bedroom 2 that is also flexible as a dining room.

❺ Separate from living and other sleeping areas, the master suite enjoys a rear covered porch in seclusion.

❻ A laundry closet is centrally located, saving time on household chores.

PLAN HPT04001

Type: One-Story
Total Square Feet: 1,191
Bedrooms: 3
Bathrooms: 2
Width: 48'-4" **Depth:** 43'-8"

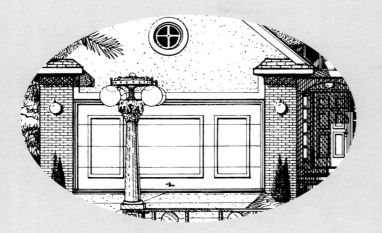

MEMORIES . . .

Stairs leading to a storage area above the garage jog memories of attic treasures in a childhood home: outgrown toys too dear to part with, a proud soldier's uniform, a yellowed wedding gown, holiday decorations and surprise gifts stored for safe keeping.

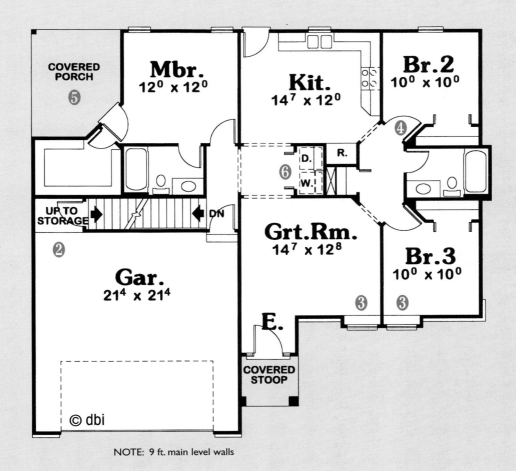

COVERED PORCH
⑤

Mbr.
12⁰ x 12⁰

Kit.
14⁷ x 12⁰

Br.2
10⁰ x 10⁰

④

UP TO STORAGE

DN

D.

R.

W.

⑥

②

Grt.Rm.
14⁷ x 12⁸

Br.3
10⁰ x 10⁰

Gar.
21⁴ x 21⁴

③

③

E.

© dbi

COVERED STOOP

NOTE: 9 ft. main level walls

THE LINDALE

1 The use of brick on the front exterior of this home offers low maintenance.

2 A large living room has plenty of room to accommodate guests and features an 11-foot ceiling and a pair of double windows surrounding the fireplace.

3 The dining room features a double window and backyard access.

4 U-shaped counters in the kitchen create an efficient work area and offer service to the living room.

5 The large master bedroom has an adjoining bath with walk-in closet and tub beneath a window.

6 Bedroom 2 offers the visual appeal of an arched window and sloped ceiling.

PLAN HPT040002

Type: One-Story
Total Square Feet: 1,395
Bedrooms: 3
Bathrooms: 2
Width: 44'-0" **Depth:** 46'-0"

MEMORIES . . .

It wasn't long ago that Dad did a lot of his own car repairs and teenage boys tinkered with old jalopies to turn them into hot rods. They crawled out from under the vehicles covered with grease and grime. A sink in the garage would have made Mom so much happier!

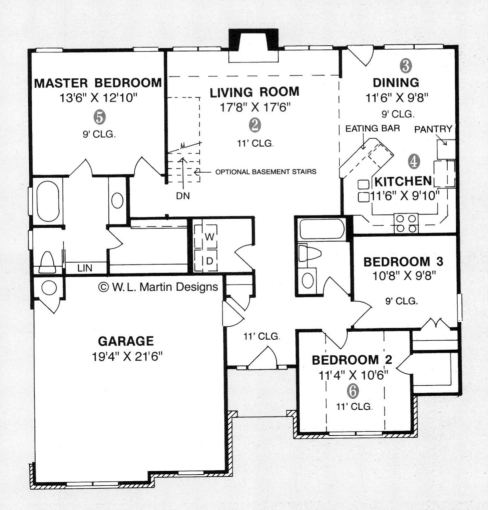

MASTER BEDROOM
13'6" X 12'10"
⑤
9' CLG.

LIVING ROOM
17'8" X 17'6"
②
11' CLG.

OPTIONAL BASEMENT STAIRS

DN

③
DINING
11'6" X 9'8"
9' CLG.

EATING BAR   PANTRY

④
KITCHEN
11'6" X 9'10"

W
D

LIN

© W. L. Martin Designs

GARAGE
19'4" X 21'6"

11' CLG.

BEDROOM 3
10'8" X 9'8"
9' CLG.

BEDROOM 2
11'4" X 10'6"
⑥
11' CLG.

THE PAYSON

1 This country cottage is updated with a hip roof and eyebrow arches.

2 Traffic flows neatly through the den just inside the entry.

3 With no wasted space, the kitchen and breakfast area function as a large living area organized with an island counter.

4 His and her walk-in closets offer plenty of practical storage options in the master suite.

5 An optional finished basement provides the possibility of creating an apartment for a live-in relative.

6 Extra bedrooms in the basement are perfect for occasional visits from friends and relatives.

PLAN HPT040003

Type: One-Story
Total Square Feet: 1,472
Bedrooms: 3
Bathrooms: 3
Width: 49'-8" **Depth:** 45'-0"

Fam. Rm.
35⁷ x 17⁶

Br.2
12⁰ x 12¹⁰

ENTERTAINMENT CENTER

⑤

Kit.
10¹⁰ x 11⁰   UP

Storage

⑥

Br.3
12⁰ x 12¹⁰

SEAT

Optional Finished Basement Plan
Adds 1169 Sq. Ft.

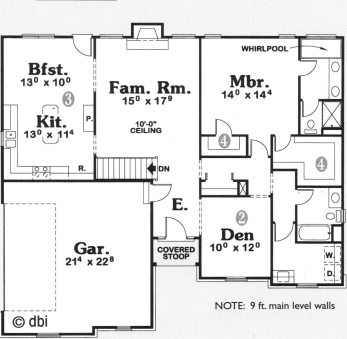

WHIRLPOOL

Bfst.
13⁰ x 10⁰

③

Kit.
13⁰ x 11⁴

P.

Fam. Rm.
15⁰ x 17⁹

10'-0"
CEILING

Mbr.
14⁰ x 14⁴

R.

DN

④

④

E.

Gar.
21⁴ x 22⁸

COVERED
STOOP

②

Den
10⁰ x 12⁰

W.
D.

© dbi

NOTE: 9 ft. main level walls

MEMORIES . . .

The huge optional family room in the basement of this home evokes memories of extended family gatherings—when we enjoyed a fabulous Thanksgiving dinner on borrowed card tables or exchanged gifts on Christmas morning.

THE KELSEY

1 A picturesque covered porch adds charm to this ranch home.

2 With an 11-foot ceiling and transom-topped windows flanking the fireplace, this great room provides a lovely view from the entry.

3 Attractive bowed breakfast area is open to kitchen with island snack bar, corner sink and access to the back yard.

4 Secondary bedrooms share a hall bath with two convenient linen closets.

5 French doors, an arched window and a 10-foot ceiling enhance the den which could also be used as a third bedroom.

6 Spacious master suite features whirlpool bath, dual lavs and mirrored doors to walk-in closets.

PLAN HPT040004

Type: One-Story
Total Square Feet: 1,479
Bedrooms: 2
Bathrooms: 2
Width: 48'-0" **Depth:** 50'-0"

MEMORIES . . .

This quaint porch reminds us of the first day of school. Mom took our picture as we stood on the porch in brand new clothes and shiny saddle shoes with a metal lunch box in one hand and a bag full of school supplies in the other.

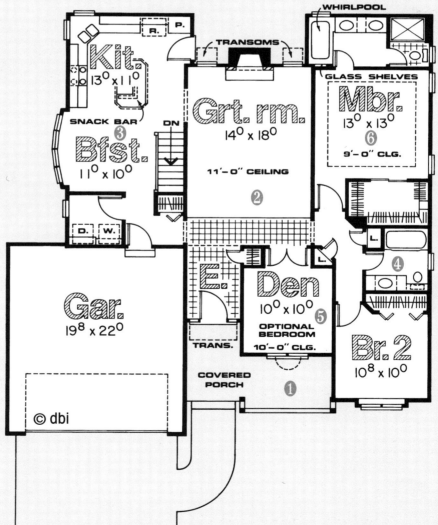

OPTIONAL BEDROOM

OPTIONAL Br.3
10^0 x 10^0
10'–0" CLG.

Kit.
13^0 x 11^0

R.   P.

TRANSOMS

Grt. rm.
14^0 x 18^0

11'–0" CEILING ②

WHIRLPOOL

GLASS SHELVES

Mbr.
13^0 x 13^0
⑥
9'–0" CLG.

SNACK BAR
③
Bfst.
11^0 x 10^0

DN

D.   W.

Gar.
19^8 x 22^0

© dbi

E.

Den
10^0 x 10^0 ⑤
OPTIONAL BEDROOM
10'–0" CLG.

TRANS.

COVERED PORCH
①

L.

④

Br.2
10^8 x 10^0

THE FELDON

① This home's front porch was meant to be used—with its 6-foot depth, 9-foot-high ceiling and large columns.

② Ten-foot-high ceilings add a sense of spaciousness to the living and dining rooms.

③ Cabinets wrap around a central island with eating bar in the kitchen.

④ The master suite enjoys a lovely angled ceiling, walk-in closet, soaking tub and double vanity.

⑤ The garage offers a walk-in storage closet.

⑥ A compartmented bath serves the three secondary bedrooms, allowing more than one person to get ready in the morning.

PLAN HPT040005

Type: One-Story
Total Square Feet: 1,539
Bedrooms: 4
Bathrooms: 2
Width: 56'-0" **Depth:** 52'-0"

MEMORIES . . .

Family vacations. Months of anticipation, planning, packing and long car rides. Whether we were fishing and camping, visiting relatives, exploring the Grand Canyon or touring Graceland... after a week or two we couldn't wait to get home. Wouldn't this be a welcoming home to come back to?

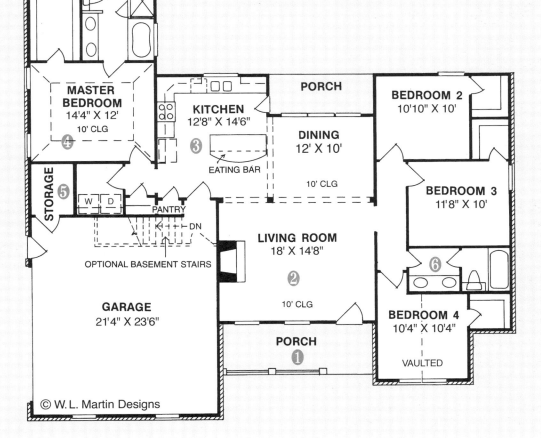

MASTER BEDROOM
14'4" X 12'
10' CLG
④

KITCHEN
12'8" X 14'6"
③

EATING BAR

PORCH

DINING
12' X 10'

10' CLG

BEDROOM 2
10'10" X 10'

STORAGE
⑤

W   D

PANTRY

DN

OPTIONAL BASEMENT STAIRS

LIVING ROOM
18' X 14'8"

②

10' CLG

BEDROOM 3
11'8" X 10'

⑥

GARAGE
21'4" X 23'6"

PORCH

①

BEDROOM 4
10'4" X 10'4"

VAULTED

© W. L. Martin Designs

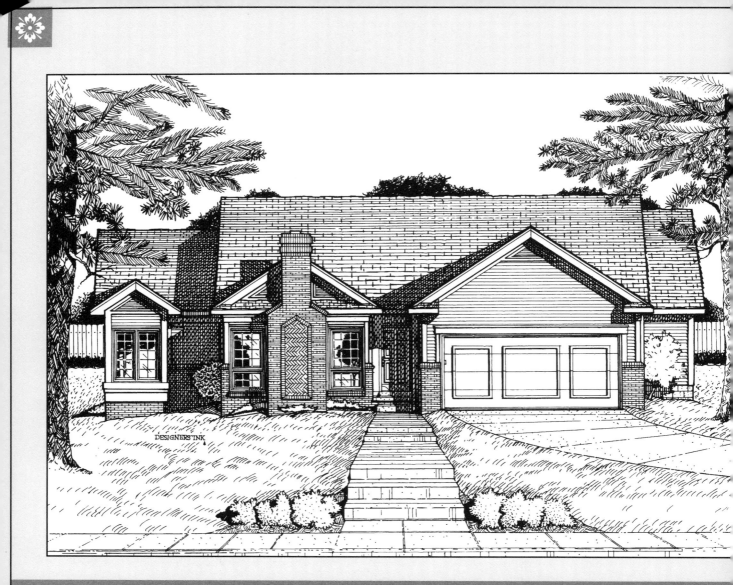

THE ASHCROFT

❶ A large pantry accompanies the kitchen with angled snack bar.

❷ Guests will have complete privacy in bedroom 2 with its own full bath and walk-in closet.

❸ A U-shaped stairway with open railing creates interest in the dining room. If not building a basement, extra space in the dining room will be especially welcome.

❹ Oak flooring throughout all living areas creates visual integration among all rooms.

❺ A large walk-in closet provides plenty of wardrobe space for the master suite.

❻ A soaking sink, hanging closet and built-in bench with hooks helps the laundry room serve dually as a mud entry.

PLAN HPT040006

Type: One-Story
Total Square Feet: 1,577
Bedrooms: 2
Bathrooms: 2½
Width: 59'-4" **Depth:** 49'-4"

Memories . . .

With a great room facing the front of the home, one remembers a simple afternoon from long ago—lying on the floor in front of the fireplace working on a puzzle, watching for Dad to come up the walk.

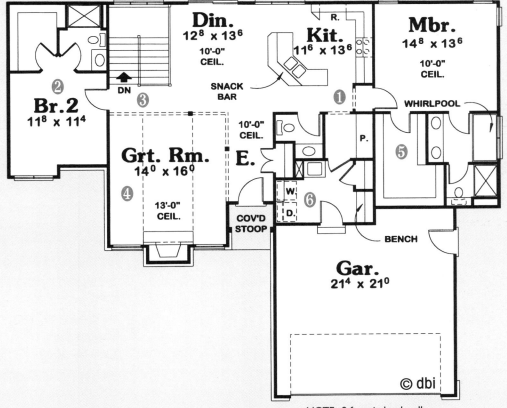

Din.
12⁸ x 13⁶

10'-0"
CEIL.

Kit.
11⁶ x 13⁶

R.

Mbr.
14⁸ x 13⁶

10'-0"
CEIL.

DN

②

Br.2
11⁸ x 11⁴

③

SNACK BAR

①

WHIRLPOOL

10'-0"
CEIL.

P.

⑤

Grt. Rm.
14⁰ x 16⁰

E.

④

13'-0"
CEIL.

W

D

⑥

COV'D STOOP

BENCH

Gar.
21⁴ x 21⁰

© dbi

NOTE: 9 ft. main level walls

THE THOMASTON

1 Traditional styling can be found in this home's moldings, corner boards and double-hung windows.

2 The dining room could easily convert into a family computer/ homework area.

3 An ample corridor leads to the bedroom wing with the master suite and two bedrooms.

4 A large walk-in closet, whirlpool and dual-lav vanity add convenience in the master bath.

5 The kitchen and dinette are well-integrated to function for everyday activity.

6 A pocket door encloses the laundry room, which includes a linen closet and soaking sink.

PLAN HPT040007

Type: One-Story
Total Square Feet: 1,660
Bedrooms: 3
Bathrooms: 2
Width: 54'-4" **Depth:** 48'-4"

MEMORIES . . .

The generous pantry in this kitchen is reminiscent of the good old days—when you bounced in the door and joyfully tossed your books on the kitchen table. The only thing on your mind was rummaging through the cupboards to see what you could find for a snack.

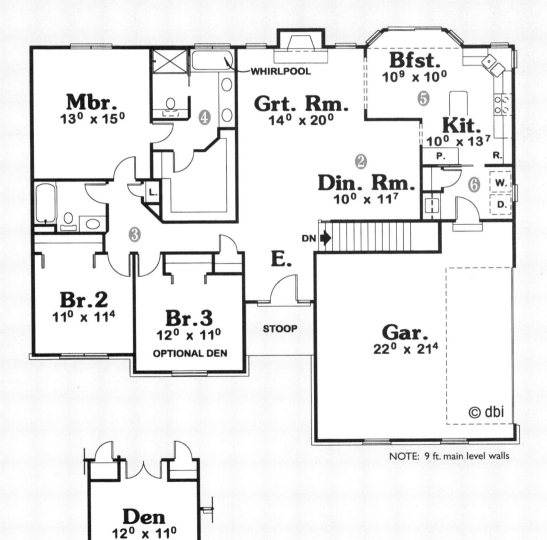

Mbr.
13⁰ x 15⁰

WHIRLPOOL

Grt. Rm.
14⁰ x 20⁰

Bfst.
10⁹ x 10⁰

Kit.
10⁰ x 13⁷

P.

R.

Din. Rm.
10⁰ x 11⁷

W.

D.

Br.2
11⁰ x 11⁴

Br.3
12⁰ x 11⁰
OPTIONAL DEN

E.

STOOP

DN

Gar.
22⁰ x 21⁴

© dbi

NOTE: 9 ft. main level walls

Den
12⁰ x 11⁰

OPTIONAL DEN

THE WAVERLY

① Ten-foot walls and elegant ceiling detail add grace to the formal dining room off the entry.

② Volume great room with raised hearth fireplace is framed by transom-topped windows.

③ In the kitchen and bowed dinette area, convenient extras include a snack bar, pantry, lazy Susan and door to the back yard.

④ Two secondary bedrooms could be converted to a sun room with French doors from the dinette and an optional den.

⑤ Bedroom 3 has a built-in desk flanked by two closets.

⑥ A secluded master suite features boxed ceiling, skylit dressing area, his and her lavs, corner whirlpool tub and roomy walk-in closet.

PLAN HPT040008

Type: One-Story
Total Square Feet: 1,710
Bedrooms: 3
Bathrooms: 2
Width: 53'-4" **Depth:** 54'-10"

MEMORIES . . .

As kids, we loved or hated bath time. Either the water was too hot for our taste and Mom scrubbed too hard with the washcloth...or, we had a great time playing in the bubbles with a toy boat or duck. A lovely whirlpool in a spacious bathroom is bound to make a bath lover out of anyone!

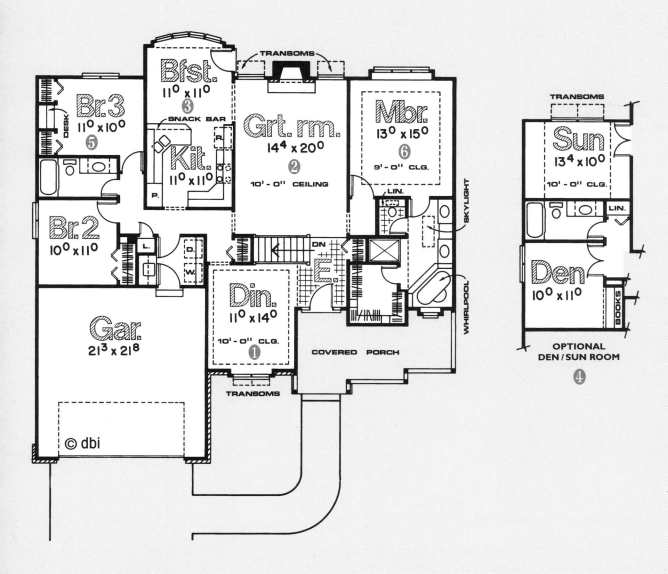

Br.3
11⁰ x 10⁰
⑤

Bfst.
11⁰ x 11⁰
③

SNACK BAR

Kit.
11⁰ x 11⁰

Grt. rm.
14⁴ x 20⁰
②
10'- 0'' CEILING

Mbr.
13⁰ x 15⁰
⑥
9'- 0'' CLG.

TRANSOMS

LIN.

SKYLIGHT

Br.2
10⁰ x 11⁰

WHIRLPOOL

Gar.
21³ x 21⁸

DN

Din.
11⁰ x 14⁰
10'- 0'' CLG.
①

© dbi

TRANSOMS

COVERED PORCH

TRANSOMS

Sun
13⁴ x 10⁰
10'- 0'' CLG.

LIN.

Den
10⁰ x 11⁰

BOOKS

OPTIONAL
DEN / SUN ROOM
④

THE BRADBURY

① The kitchen has a snack bar, breakfast area and pantry and is near a convenient laundry room off the garage.

② A stairway to the lower level and an 11-foot ceiling make the large great room seem even larger.

③ Along with angled entries, bedrooms 2 and 3 enjoy roomy closets and access to a full bath.

④ The entry opens dramatically to an impressive volume great room.

⑤ The master suite welcomes a shower and whirlpool tub, dual lavs, compartmented stool and a large walk-in closet.

⑥ A rear covered stoop makes a perfect garden center or sitting porch.

PLAN HPT040009

Type: One-Story
Total Square Feet: 1,758
Bedrooms: 3
Bathrooms: 2
Width: 55'-4" **Depth:** 49'-8"

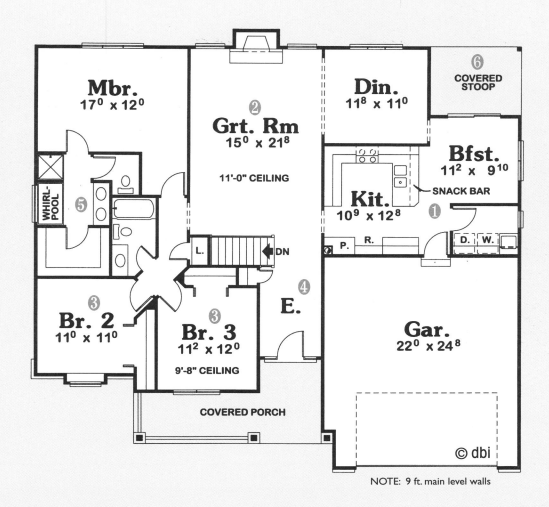

Mbr.
17⁰ x 12⁰

② **Grt. Rm**
15⁰ x 21⁸

11'-0" CEILING

⑤ WHIRL-POOL

③ **Br. 2**
11⁰ x 11⁰

③ **Br. 3**
11² x 12⁰

9'-8" CEILING

L.

DN

④ **E.**

COVERED PORCH

Din.
11⁸ x 11⁰

⑥ COVERED STOOP

Bfst.
11² x 9¹⁰

SNACK BAR

① **Kit.**
10⁹ x 12⁸

P. R.

D. W.

Gar.
22⁰ x 24⁸

© dbi

NOTE: 9 ft. main level walls

MEMORIES . . .

Patio doors in the breakfast area lead to a covered stoop much like the one you sat on with your childhood friends licking drippy popsicles, spitting watermelon seeds and eating cupcakes with sticky frosting.

THE ANANDALE

1 A friendly walk-thru kitchen is well-integrated with the dinette and features an island snack bar.

2 For convenience, a rear covered porch accesses both the great room and breakfast area.

3 A large attic upstairs lends itself to a hobby room or an extra bedroom suite.

4 Bedroom 2 features a walk-in closet and is across from a full bath.

5 French doors reveal the master bath with tempting whirlpool tub, dual-lav vanity and convenient walk-in closet.

6 A front porch lends the feel of times gone by on this Cape Cod-inspired elevation.

PLAN HPT040010

Type: One-Story
Total Square Feet: 1,768
Bedrooms: 2
Bathrooms: 2
Width: 72'-8" **Depth:** 42'-0"

MEMORIES . . .

Grandma's sewing room was a magical place where she created ruffled curtains, lacy Easter dresses, cowboy vests, Superman capes and elaborate Halloween costumes. This home's attic could be turned into a hobby area for all of your special projects.

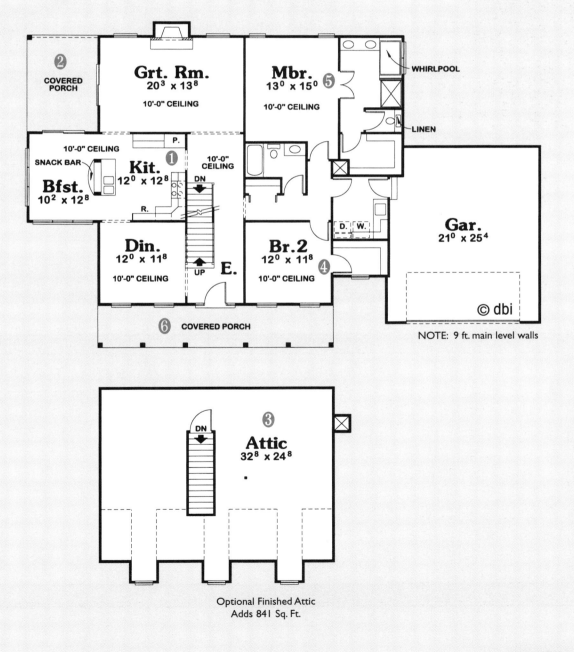

2 COVERED PORCH

Grt. Rm. 20^3 x 13^8
10'-0" CEILING

Mbr. 13^0 x 15^0 **5**
10'-0" CEILING

WHIRLPOOL

LINEN

10'-0" CEILING

P.

SNACK BAR

Bfst. 10^2 x 12^8

Kit. 12^0 x 12^8 **1**

10'-0" CEILING

DN

R.

Din. 12^0 x 11^8
10'-0" CEILING

UP

E.

Br.2 12^0 x 11^8 **4**
10'-0" CEILING

D. W.

Gar. 21^0 x 25^4

© dbi

NOTE: 9 ft. main level walls

6 COVERED PORCH

DN

3

Attic 32^8 x 24^8

Optional Finished Attic
Adds 841 Sq. Ft.

THE BENNETT

PLAN HPT040011

1. Arched windows and a volume ceiling in the dining room capture the eye upon entry.

2. Hearth area has bayed windows and shares a 3-sided fireplace.

3. The kitchen is equipped with a snack bar peninsula, large pantry and lazy Susan.

4. Picture awning windows flood the breakfast area with light.

5. Special features in the master suite include a 9-foot ceiling, large walk-in closet and whirlpool tub.

6. Two secondary bedrooms are in a separate wing for added privacy.

Type: One-Story
Total Square Feet: 1,782
Bedrooms: 3
Bathrooms: 2
Width: 52'-0" **Depth:** 59'-4"

MEMORIES . . .

This lovely covered stoop brings back memories of trick-or-treating on Halloween. Wearing super hero costumes or frilly princess gowns, we ran from house to house filling our bags of goodies. And it was the one night of the year that Mom let us eat all the candy we wanted.

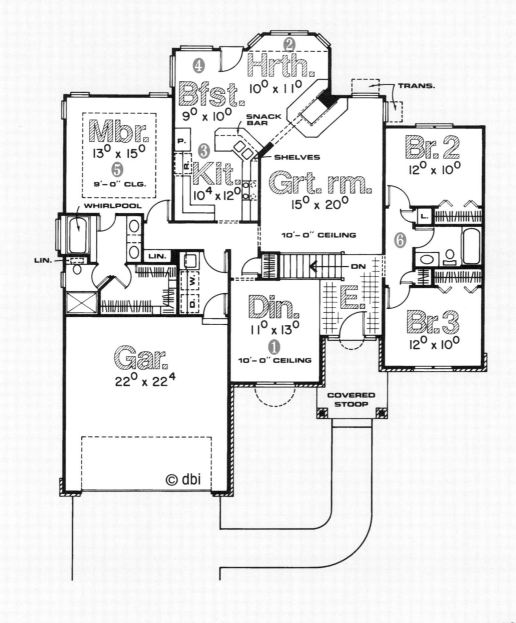

Hrth.
10⁰ x 11⁰

Bfst.
9⁰ x 10⁰

SNACK BAR

TRANS.

Mbr.
13⁰ x 15⁰
9'-0" CLG.

P.

SHELVES

Kit.
10⁴ x 12⁰

Grt. rm.
15⁰ x 20⁰
10'-0" CEILING

Br. 2
12⁰ x 10⁰

WHIRLPOOL

LIN.

LIN.

D. W.

L.

DN

Gar.
22⁰ x 22⁴

Din.
11⁰ x 13⁰
10'-0" CEILING

E.

Br. 3
12⁰ x 10⁰

COVERED STOOP

© dbi

THE CHRISTINE

① Both secondary bedrooms are separated from the master suite and readily access a full bath.

② A large storage area in the garage can be used to place garden and lawn equipment.

③ Built-in benches in the entry and master suite walk-in closet help assist removing shoes and getting ready for the day.

④ The central location and integration of the kitchen, great room and breakfast area caters to the modern family's lifestyle.

⑤ A covered porch off the master suite can help couples catch up on their day in privacy.

⑥ A coffered ceiling defines the perimeter of the dining room with beautiful view to the front.

PLAN HPT040012

Type: One-Story
Total Square Feet: 1,790
Bedrooms: 3
Bathrooms: 2
Width: 55'-0"   **Depth:** 57'-0"

MEMORIES . . .

A long snack bar accessible to the great room brings back thoughts of carefree evenings watching Mr. Ed, Bonanza, Gilligan's Island and The Andy Griffith Show—snacking on fresh popcorn, chips and dip or roasted peanuts in the shell.

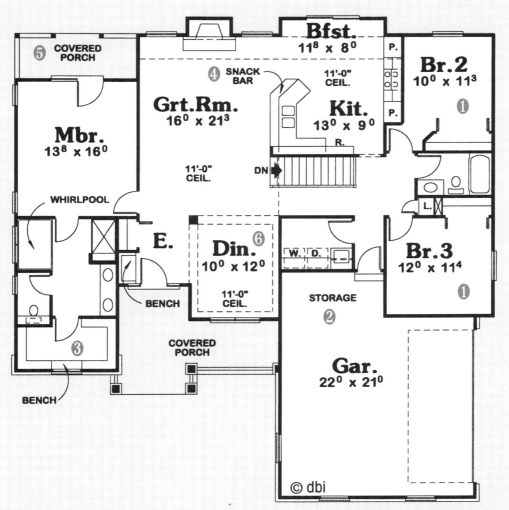

⑤ COVERED PORCH

Bfst.
11⁸ x 8⁰

P.

Br. 2
10⁰ x 11³

①

④ SNACK BAR

11'-0" CEIL.

Grt. Rm.
16⁰ x 21³

Kit.
13⁰ x 9⁰

P.

Mbr.
13⁸ x 16⁰

11'-0" CEIL.

R.

WHIRLPOOL

DN

L.

E.

Din.
10⁰ x 12⁰

⑥

W. D.

Br. 3
12⁰ x 11⁴

BENCH

11'-0" CEIL.

STORAGE ②

①

③

COVERED PORCH

Gar.
22⁰ x 21⁰

BENCH

© dbi

NOTE: 9 ft. main level walls

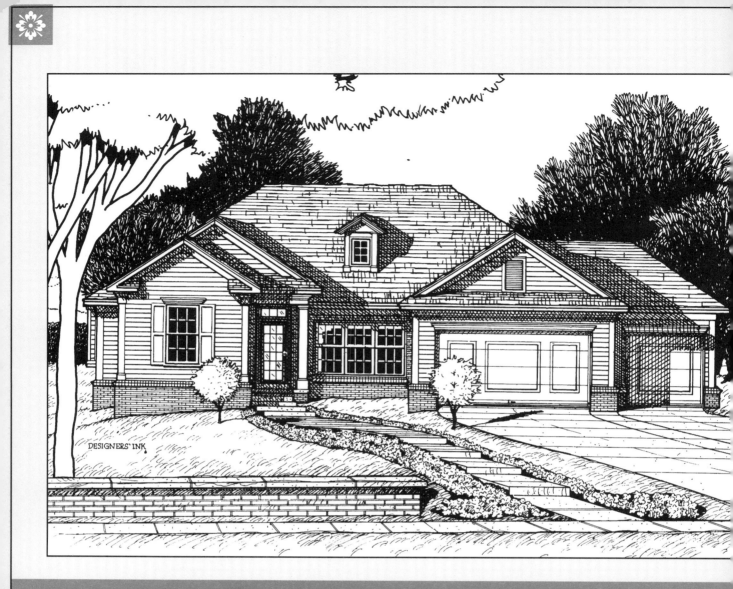

DESIGNERS' INK

THE VAUTRIN

① Formal meals in the dining room will be easy with a nearby servery.

② An angled snack bar in the kitchen offers service to both the breakfast area and great room.

③ Deep window sills create a picturesque atmosphere in the breakfast area.

④ Just off the dinette, a covered porch is a great place to relax in the evening.

⑤ A third bedroom is functional as a den and is within steps of a full bath with linen closet.

⑥ A volume ceiling adds even more spaciousness to the pampering master suite.

PLAN HPT040013

Type: One-Story
Total Square Feet: 1,806
Bedrooms: 3
Bathrooms: 2
Width: 65'-4" **Depth:** 56'-0"

MEMORIES . . .

*Celebrations have always revolved
around food. On the 4th of July, it was
homemade ice cream. Easter meant
baked ham and a bunny-face cake.
Valentine's day—fancy, heart-shaped
cookies. For Christmas it was fudge and
divinity. What better place to create
those goodies than this spacious kitchen?*

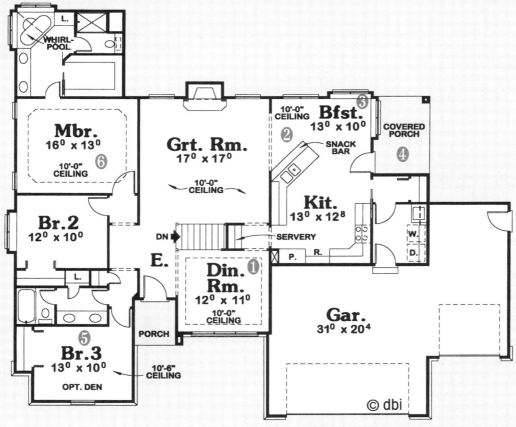

WHIRL-
POOL

L.

Mbr.
16⁰ x 13⁰
10'-0"
CEILING
6

Grt. Rm.
17⁰ x 17⁰
10'-0"
CEILING

10'-0"
CEILING
Bfst.
13⁰ x 10⁰
3

2

SNACK
BAR

COVERED
PORCH
4

Br.2
12⁰ x 10⁰

Kit.
13⁰ x 12⁸

DN

SERVERY

E.

L.

Din.
Rm.
12⁰ x 11⁰
10'-0"
CEILING
1

P.   R.

W.

D.

PORCH

Gar.
31⁰ x 20⁴

5

Br.3
13⁰ x 10⁰
10'-6"
CEILING

OPT. DEN

© dbi

NOTE: 9 ft. main level walls

THE SHAWNEE

❶ In the kitchen and breakfast area, wrapping counters, a desk, work island and wet bar/servery make entertaining easier.

❷ A ten-foot high entry with view to the great room provides impact.

❸ Transom-topped windows, a boxed ceiling, special hutch space and column add drama in the dining room.

❹ Just off the garage, the laundry doubles as a mud room with sink, window and extra counter space.

❺ Bedroom 2 could easily be converted to a den with French doors off the entry.

❻ The master suite enjoys a decorative boxed ceiling, dual lavs, walk-in closet, whirlpool and cedar-lined window seat for storage.

PLAN HPT040014

Type: One-Story
Total Square Feet: 1,850
Bedrooms: 3
Bathrooms: 2
Width: 62'-0" **Depth:** 48'-0"

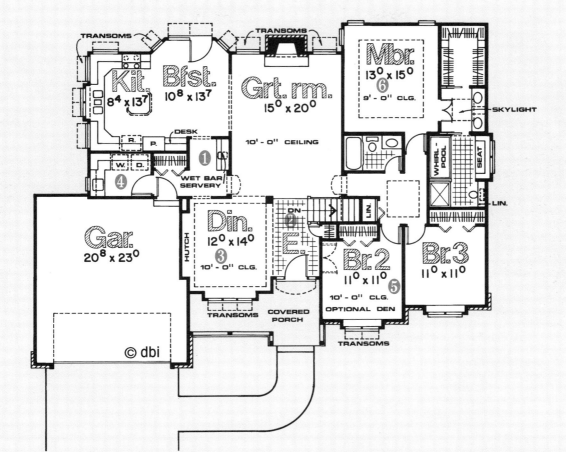

Kit.
8⁴ x 13⁷

Bfst.
10⁸ x 13⁷

Grt. rm.
15⁰ x 20⁰

10' - 0'' CEILING

Mbr.
13⁰ x 15⁰
⑥
9' - 0'' CLG.

TRANSOMS

TRANSOMS

SKYLIGHT

WHIRL-POOL

SEAT

DESK

R.

P.

①

WET BAR
SERVERY

W.   D.

④

LIN.

Gar.
20⁸ x 23⁰

© dbi

HUTCH

Din.
12⁰ x 14⁰
③
10' - 0'' CLG.

DN

②

LIN.

Br.2
11⁰ x 11⁰
⑤
10' - 0'' CLG.
OPTIONAL DEN

Br.3
11⁰ x 11⁰

TRANSOMS

COVERED
PORCH

TRANSOMS

MEMORIES . . .

Grandma's hutch was filled with "untouchables." The antique glassware that belonged to her mother, the china plates she got for her wedding, the sterling silver tea set her children bought for her 25th wedding anniversary. This dining room features a special spot for a hutch with your prized possessions.

THE MORENCI

❶ Corner boards and squared columns accent this enchanting one-story home.

❷ The large great room is ideally suited to accommodate guests from the entry as well as the dining room.

❸ An angled snack bar in the kitchen makes a great place for an informal meal.

❹ Perfect as a den or in-law suite, bedroom 4 is secluded and offers a ³/₄ bath and walk-in closet.

❺ On the opposite end of the home, the master bedroom is organized with a compartmented shower and dressing area.

❻ Two secondary bedrooms easily accommodate guests or a hobby, such as sewing.

PLAN HPT040015

Type: One-Story
Total Square Feet: 1,853
Bedrooms: 4
Bathrooms: 3
Width: 52'-8" **Depth:** 59'-0"

MEMORIES . . .

The wide open spaces in the great room bring back images of Dad giving wild piggy back rides, demonstrating wrestling holds, proving he could stand on his head and displaying his magnificent shadow boxing technique.

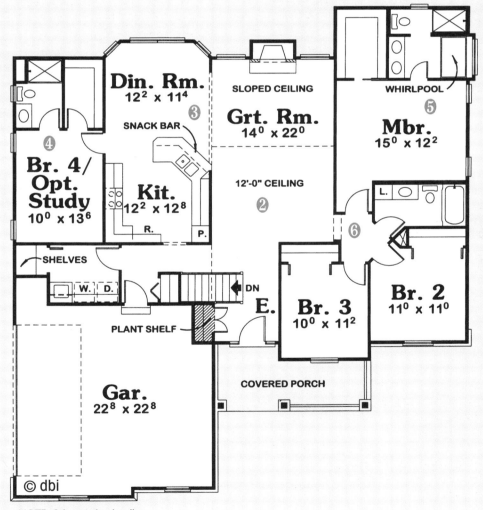

Din. Rm.
12^2 x 11^4

SLOPED CEILING

Grt. Rm.
14^0 x 22^0

WHIRLPOOL

Mbr.
15^0 x 12^2

SNACK BAR

③

Br. 4/ Opt. Study
10^0 x 13^6

④

Kit.
12^2 x 12^8

12'-0" CEILING

②

⑤

L.

R.

P.

⑥

SHELVES

W. D.

DN

E.

PLANT SHELF

Br. 3
10^0 x 11^2

Br. 2
11^0 x 11^0

Gar.
22^8 x 22^8

© dbi

COVERED PORCH

NOTE: 9 ft. main level walls

THE SUMMERWOOD

1 The entry provides an open view of a lovely dining room with special ceiling detail and a large boxed window.

2 Highlights in the great room include a 3-sided see-thru fireplace and built-in entertainment center and bookcases.

3 Bay windowed hearth room with ten-foot ceiling and see-thru fireplace offers a cozy retreat.

4 Ample counter space, a snack bar and pantry simplify life in the kitchen and breakfast area.

5 Bedroom 2 is enhanced by a window seat framed by closets; bedroom 3 can be converted to an optional den.

6 A private master suite enjoys a sloped ceiling, skylit dressing area with his and her lavs, corner whirlpool and large walk-in closet.

PLAN HPT040016

Type: One-Story
Total Square Feet: 2,015
Bedrooms: 3
Bathrooms: 2
Width: 56'-0" **Depth:** 61'-4"

③ **Hrth.**
12^0 x 12^0
10' - 0"
CLG.

TRANSOMS

SEAT

⑤ **Br.2**
12^0 x 12^5

Bfst.
11^0 x 10^0

④

SNACK BAR

TRANSOMS

P.

R.

Grt. rm.
17^2 x 20^3

② ENT. CENTER

BOOKS

Mbr.
13^0 x 15^0

⑥

9' - 8"
CEILING

Kit.
12^0 x 10^8

LIN.

10' - 0" CEILING

SKYLIGHT

⑤ **Den**
12^0 x 12^0

BOOKS

OPTIONAL DEN

Br.3
12^0 x 12^0

L.

D. W.

DN

Din.
13^0 x 13^2
9' - 4" CLG.

① E.

WHIRLPOOL

Gar.
21^3 x 21^8

TRANS.

COVERED PORCH

© dbi

MEMORIES . . .

A built-in entertainment center stirs memories of times the family gathered around the television set to watch events we'd never forget: Neil Armstrong walking on the moon, the Beatles' first appearance on the Ed Sullivan show, the "Miracle on Ice" from the 1980 Olympics.

THE CREIGHTON

1 Attractive columns, an angled garage and a stucco veneer dignify this eye-catching one-story home.

2 A feeling of tranquillity rests in the great room featuring a see-thru fireplace, entertainment center and French doors leading to a covered back porch.

3 Extra space in the master bedroom provides a place for sitting or work area.

4 The see-thru fireplace creates a comfortable atmosphere for working in the kitchen, which also boasts a walk-in pantry and huge snack bar.

5 Two covered rear porches encourage relaxation, and offer fun opportunities for outdoor activities.

6 An angled garage makes the home useable on a narrower lot.

PLAN HPT040017

Type: One-Story
Total Square Feet: 2,057
Bedrooms: 3
Bathrooms: 2
Width: 73'-4" **Depth:** 56'-8"

MEMORIES . . .

Remember when you knew your neighbors? The grown-ups stopped in for coffee or got together to play Canasta. The kids played hide 'n seek or backyard football. With two covered porches, it wouldn't be hard to have a backyard barbecue and get to know the people who live next door.

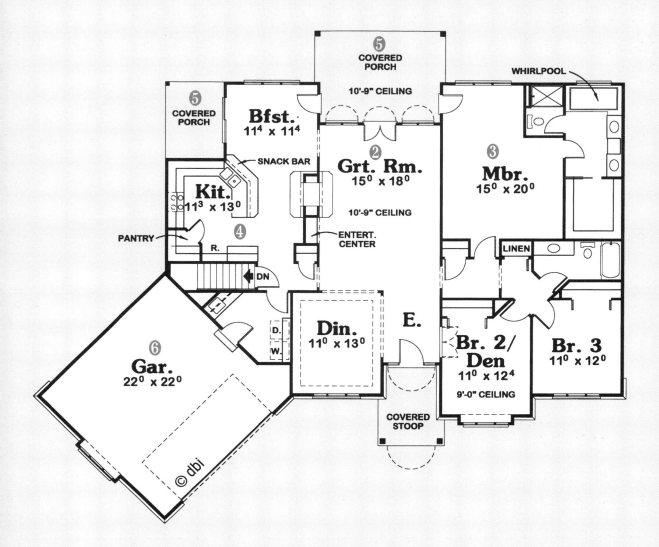

5
COVERED
PORCH

10'-9" CEILING

WHIRLPOOL

5
COVERED
PORCH

Bfst.
11⁴ x 11⁴

SNACK BAR

2 **Grt. Rm.**
15⁰ x 18⁰

3
Mbr.
15⁰ x 20⁰

Kit.
11³ x 13⁰

10'-9" CEILING

PANTRY

4

ENTERT.
CENTER

R.

LINEN

DN

Din.
11⁰ x 13⁰

E.

6
Gar.
22⁰ x 22⁰

D.

W.

**Br. 2/
Den**
11⁰ x 12⁴

9'-0" CEILING

Br. 3
11⁰ x 12⁰

COVERED
STOOP

© dbi

THE CLARKSON

① This sprawling plantation style home is characterized by its extensive front porch and triple dormers resting on its gable roofline.

② A 12-foot-high ceiling in the entry steps down to 11 feet in the adjacent living and dining rooms.

③ A built-in entertainment center in the family room offers an ideal place for home electronics.

④ A three-sided fireplace brings warmth to the kitchen, breakfast nook and family room.

⑤ The master bedroom is positioned away from two additional bedrooms and has room for a pair of chairs beside its bayed window.

⑥ Front and rear porches are great places to enjoy leisure time.

PLAN HPT040018

Type: One-Story
Total Square Feet: 2,126
Bedrooms: 3
Bathrooms: 2
Width: 66'-0" **Depth:** 54'-0"

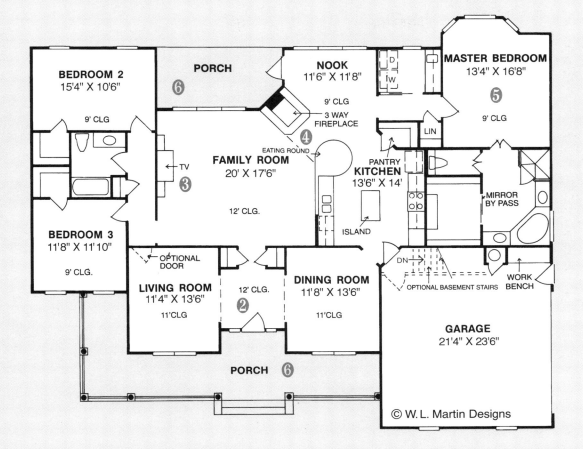

BEDROOM 2
15'4" X 10'6"

9' CLG

PORCH
⑥

NOOK
11'6" X 11'8"

9' CLG

3 WAY
FIREPLACE

MASTER BEDROOM
13'4" X 16'8"

⑤

9' CLG

EATING ROUND

④

FAMILY ROOM
20' X 17'6"

← TV

③

12' CLG.

PANTRY

KITCHEN
13'6" X 14'

LIN

MIRROR
BY PASS

ISLAND

BEDROOM 3
11'8" X 11'10"

9' CLG.

← OPTIONAL
DOOR

LIVING ROOM
11'4" X 13'6"

12' CLG.

②

11'CLG

DINING ROOM
11'8" X 13'6"

11'CLG

DN

OPTIONAL BASEMENT STAIRS

WORK
BENCH

GARAGE
21'4" X 23'6"

PORCH ⑥

© W. L. Martin Designs

Memories . . .

Remember when you clamored for your mother's attention? "Watch me!" you shouted before doing a crooked somersault. "See how high I can swing?" "Look how far I can kick the football." The porch on the back of this home would be a perfect place to watch children play.

THE CAMERON

1 A Prairie influence brings refreshing symmetry to the front elevation.

2 Perfect for a walk-out lot situation, a stairway in the great room leads to the lower level and is open to two-story-high windows with a view to the back.

3 Separated for privacy, two secondary bedrooms share a full bath.

4 A three-sided stone fireplace brings warmth to the spacious kitchen, dinette and great room.

5 The master suite provides ample closet space and twin lavs across from a whirlpool tub.

6 Depending on the need, a den or dining room can be located just inside the entry.

PLAN HPT040019

Type: One-Story
Total Square Feet: 2,167
Bedrooms: 3
Bathrooms: 2
Width: 55'-4" **Depth:** 61'-4"

OPEN TO BELOW

DN

10'-0" CEILING

Bfst.
16¹¹ x 13⁴

②

④ **BUILT-IN**

3-SIDED FIREPLACE

Grt. Rm.
17⁰ x 17⁰

Kit.
14³ x 14⁴

P.

R.

10'-0" CEILING

WHIRL-POOL

Br.2
11⁰ x 11⁰

③

E.

⑤

Mbr.
14⁰ x 17²

⑥

Den
11⁰ x 13⁰

OPT. DINING RM.

L.

W.

D.

Br.3
11⁰ x 11⁰

Gar.
22⁸ x 22⁴

© dbi

NOTE: 9 ft. main level walls

MEMORIES . . .

This three-sided fireplace kindles three times the memories: the time the electricity was off and the whole family huddled around the fireplace playing cards by candlelight; the time Grandma and Grandpa let you roast marshmallows over it; the time you walked in on Mom and Dad snuggling in front of it.

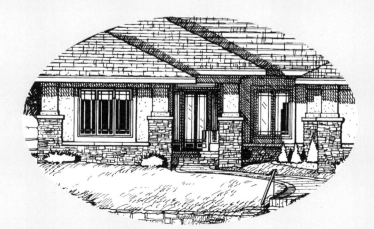

THE HARTWELL

1 Truly a retreat, the master suite offers a private sitting area, covered porch, his and her walk-in closets, separate vanities and a corner whirlpool tub.

2 The kitchen offers the advantage of a snack bar that serves both the breakfast area and great room.

3 A three-car garage provides added room for storage or a third vehicle.

4 A corner fireplace leaves an opportunity for three tall windows to fill the great room with a stunning rear view.

5 Roomy secondary bedrooms welcome additional furniture for guests and homework.

6 The front porch offers useable space for a table and a second access point into the home.

PLAN HPT040020

Type: One-Story
Total Square Feet: 2,188
Bedrooms: 3
Bathrooms: 2
Width: 74'-0" **Depth:** 49'-4"

MEMORIES . . .

Having your own car was a dream come true. It was your ticket to freedom, a symbol of your growing independence. The only hassle was moving it out of the driveway every time Mom or Dad needed to get in or out of the garage. Having a 3-car garage would have made life much simpler.

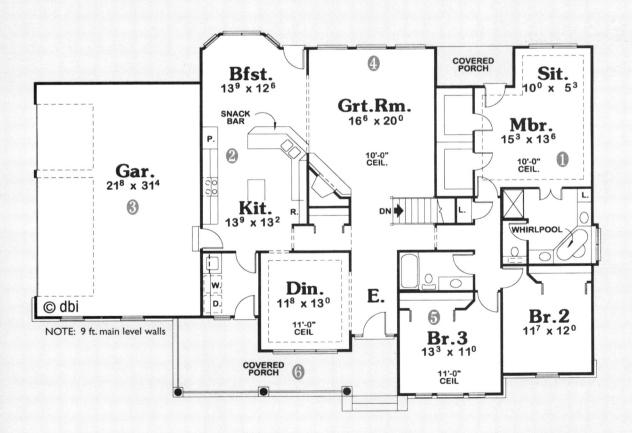

Bfst.
13⁹ x 12⁶

SNACK
BAR

P.

Grt.Rm.
16⁶ x 20⁰

COVERED
PORCH

Sit.
10⁰ x 5³

Mbr.
15³ x 13⁶

10'-0"
CEIL.

10'-0"
CEIL.

❷

Gar.
21⁸ x 31⁴

❸

Kit.
13⁹ x 13²

R.

DN

L.

L.

WHIRLPOOL

© dbi

NOTE: 9 ft. main level walls

W.

D.

Din.
11⁸ x 13⁰

11'-0"
CEIL

E.

Br.3
13³ x 11⁰

11'-0"
CEIL

Br.2
11⁷ x 12⁰

❺

COVERED
PORCH

❻

THE HOLDEN

1 The entry opens immediately to a dining room and a great room, both offering ample space for entertaining.

2 Secluded down a hall is a private office, providing the option of becoming a fourth bedroom.

3 The kitchen and breakfast area open to the great room, and have a convenient island, planning desk and pantry.

4 Perfect for individual desires, bedroom 3 could easily convert to a formal living room.

5 The master suite is also privately situated in the left wing and has a large walk-in closet, dual lavs and a compartmented stool and shower.

6 Plenty of storage space in the garage forms the perfect work alcove.

PLAN HPT040021

Type: One-Story
Total Square Feet: 2,227
Bedrooms: 4
Bathrooms: 3
Width: 76'-8" **Depth:** 48'-8"

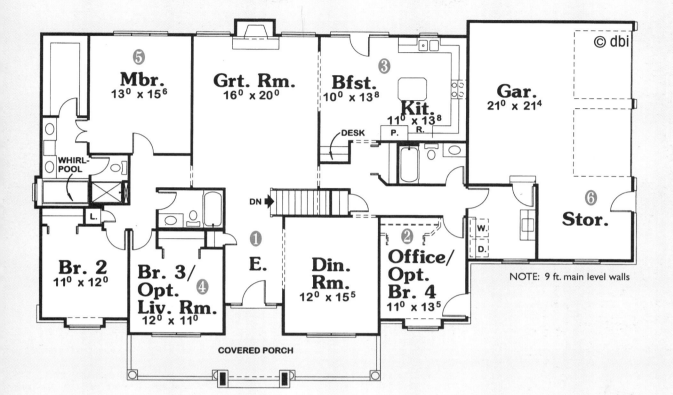

Mbr.
13⁰ x 15⁶

Grt. Rm.
16⁰ x 20⁰

Bfst.
10⁰ x 13⁸

Kit.
11⁰ x 13⁸

Gar.
21⁰ x 21⁴

© dbi

⑤

③

WHIRL-POOL

DESK

P.   R.

W.
D.

⑥

Stor.

DN ➤

①

E.

②

Br. 2
11⁰ x 12⁰

**Br. 3/
Opt.
Liv. Rm.**
12⁰ x 11⁰

④

**Din.
Rm.**
12⁰ x 15⁵

**Office/
Opt.
Br. 4**
11⁰ x 13⁵

NOTE: 9 ft. main level walls

COVERED PORCH

MEMORIES . . .

*This spacious great room seems big
enough to be a dance floor-and calls to
mind tender recollections of Dad
twirling Mom around the living room
or Mom teaching your oldest brother
how to two-step.*

THE BRIARTON

❶ Columns and dropped soffits frame a view into the living room and the backyard beyond.

❷ An integrated family room, breakfast area and kitchen will help the family circulate easily.

❸ A sitting area adjoins the master bedroom, offering a place to work in the evening or relax while enjoying a view of the back yard.

❹ A walk-in linen closet services the secondary bedrooms and nearby full bath.

❺ Extra vanity space in the master bath offers ample space to apply makeup and style hair.

❻ A utility entry from the garage accesses a useful closet, an island kitchen and an accommodating laundry room with porch.

PLAN HPT040022

Type: One-Story
Total Square Feet: 2,586
Bedrooms: 3
Bathrooms: 2 ½
Width: 72'-8" **Depth:** 64'-8"

MEMORIES . . .

Imagine how much simpler your childhood would have been with an outside door to the laundry room and a door from the garage to a coat closet. The perfect setup for removing soccer cleats, muddy tennis shoes, soggy hats and mittens or a dirty football uniform.

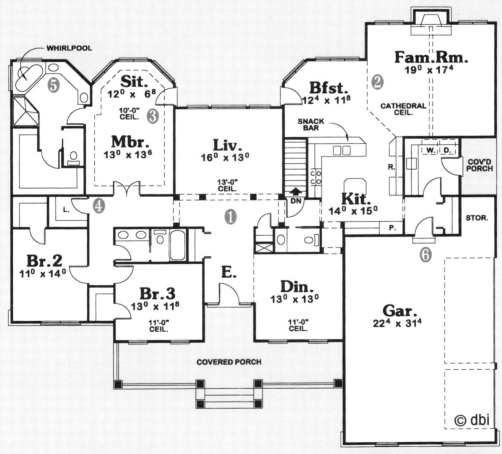

WHIRLPOOL

Sit.
$12^0 \times 6^8$

Fam.Rm.
$19^0 \times 17^4$

Bfst.
$12^4 \times 11^8$

CATHEDRAL CEIL.

10'-0" CEIL.

Mbr.
$13^0 \times 13^6$

Liv.
$16^0 \times 13^0$

SNACK BAR

13'-0" CEIL.

DN

W. D.

COV'D PORCH

R.

Kit.
$14^0 \times 15^0$

L.

STOR.

Br.2
$11^0 \times 14^0$

E.

Br.3
$13^0 \times 11^8$

11'-0" CEIL.

Din.
$13^0 \times 13^0$

11'-0" CEIL.

P.

Gar.
$22^4 \times 31^4$

© dbi

COVERED PORCH

NOTE: 9 ft. main level walls

THE LAUREN

❶ For those who work at home or catch up on office work in the evenings, a den is located just off the entry.

❷ A covered porch expands the breakfast area.

❸ Daily interaction will be effortless through the open design of the kitchen and family room.

❹ Built-in bookshelves in the master suite's sitting room help create an air of relaxation.

❺ Bedrooms 2 and 3 share a handy compartmented bath with two vanities.

❻ A convenient storage niche in the garage is ideal for creating shelves or a closet.

PLAN HPT040023

Type: One-Story
Total Square Feet: 2,650
Bedrooms: 3
Bathrooms: 2 ½
Width: 76'-0" **Depth:** 60'-8"

MEMORIES . . .

There was something so special about the moments your parents spent reading to you. Learning about the world as you sat side by side enjoying their undivided attention. Who can look at this family room with bookcases on each side of the fireplace without reminiscing about those happy times?

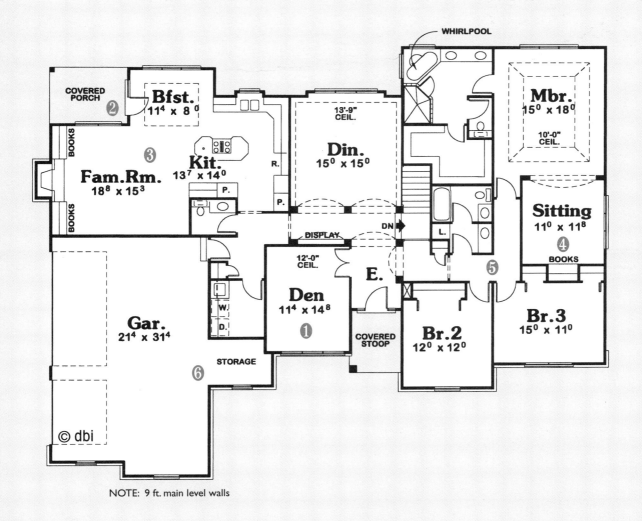

WHIRLPOOL

COVERED PORCH ❷

Bfst.
11⁴ x 8⁰

BOOKS

Fam.Rm.
18⁸ x 15³

❸

Kit.
13⁷ x 14⁰

R.

P.

P.

BOOKS

Din.
15⁰ x 15⁰

13'-9"
CEIL.

Mbr.
15⁰ x 18⁰

10'-0"
CEIL.

DN

DISPLAY

12'-0"
CEIL.

Den
11⁴ x 14⁸

❶

E.

L.

Sitting
11⁰ x 11⁸

❹

BOOKS

❺

Gar.
21⁴ x 31⁴

W.

D.

COVERED STOOP

Br.2
12⁰ x 12⁰

Br.3
15⁰ x 11⁰

STORAGE

❻

© dbi

NOTE: 9 ft. main level walls

THE SAYBROOKE

① The tapered columns, panel shutters and beautiful arched window treatments of this design offer an influential first impression.

② Just off the entry, the dining room features double doors that link to the kitchen for serving ease.

③ The kitchen, with an island and snack bar, serves the breakfast area and great room.

④ An 11-foot-high ceiling and raised hearth fireplace distinguish the great room.

⑤ Bedrooms 2 and 3 are located in the left wing of the home and share a Hollywood bath.

⑥ Bedroom 4—a perfect guest suite—easily converts into a den with double doors off the entry.

PLAN HPT040024

Type: One-Story
Total Square Feet: 2,750
Bedrooms: 4
Bathrooms: 3 ½
Width: 66'-8" **Depth:** 72'-8"

MEMORIES . . .

Remember baby sitting? It wasn't long after your "employers" left that you moseyed to their kitchen to see what they had for snacks. Every once in awhile, you hit a home where the cupboards were bare. With three pantries, this kitchen is bound to be a babysitter's dream.

Bfst.
12⁰ x 12⁴

11'-0" CEILING

DESK

SNACK BAR

Br.2
12⁰ x 12⁰

⑤

④

Grt. Rm.
16⁰ x 23⁴

11'-0" CEILING

③

Kit.
14⁰ x 14⁴

Mbr.
17⁰ x 14⁷

P.

P.

R.

P.

WHIRL-POOL

L.

Br.3
12⁰ x 12⁰

L.

DN

W.

D.

11'-0" CEILING

⑥

Br.4/
Opt. Den
12⁰ x 14⁰

E.

②

Din. Rm.
12⁰ x 16⁰

COVERED PORCH

Gar.
22⁰ x 31⁰

© dbi

NOTE: 9 ft. main level walls

In the
Nostalgia *Collection you will find...*

REAR CLOSETS

The garage entry in a home is probably one area that is most taken for granted. Its function and design are crucial in a home, but it's an area that most people don't take time to think about. One important element to its functional design is the size and availability of a back closet for the storage of coats and shoes. In a number of these designs we paid careful attention to make sure a back closet was readily available and of adequate size for the home.

SIMPLIFIED CEILING PATTERNS

In keeping with the traditional appeal of homes from the turn of the century, we simplified the ceiling patterns in the group of designs. Our design intent was to replicate the tall, flat ceilings from homes of this area. But this is also beneficial to both builders and home buyers because a flat ceiling helps save them cost. It also allows them to easily select their own ceiling pattern if they so desire.

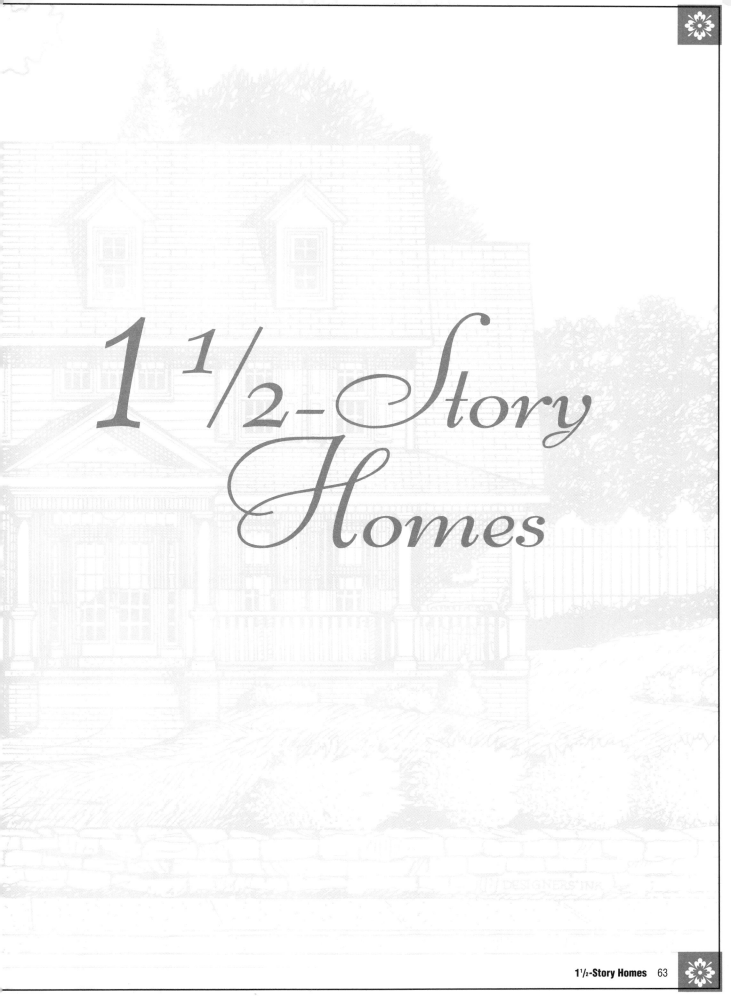

1 1/2-Story Homes

THE WINDOM

1 Special details in the living room include an 18-foot-high ceiling, a fireplace and plenty of windows.

2 An efficient kitchen shares an angled counter top with a large dining area.

3 A wrap-around porch on the back of the home is accessed from the dining room and the master bedroom.

4 Bedroom 3 features a 10-foot-high sloped ceiling and special window detail.

5 This roomy loft area, with a magnificent view down to the living room, makes a great spot for reading or computer work.

6 Two windows provide light in the roomy unfinished storage area over the garage.

PLAN HPT040025

Type: 1½-Story
First Floor: 1,029 square feet
Second Floor: 489 square feet
Total: 1,518 square feet
Bedrooms: 3
Bathrooms: 2½
Width: 44'-8" **Depth:** 59'-0"

MEMORIES . . .

Looking at this home's cozy appearance, you can almost hear voices reflecting everyday family life: "Honey, I'm home." "It's time to eat; are your hands clean?" "Finish your homework." "Is your room picked up?" "Good night. I love you, too."

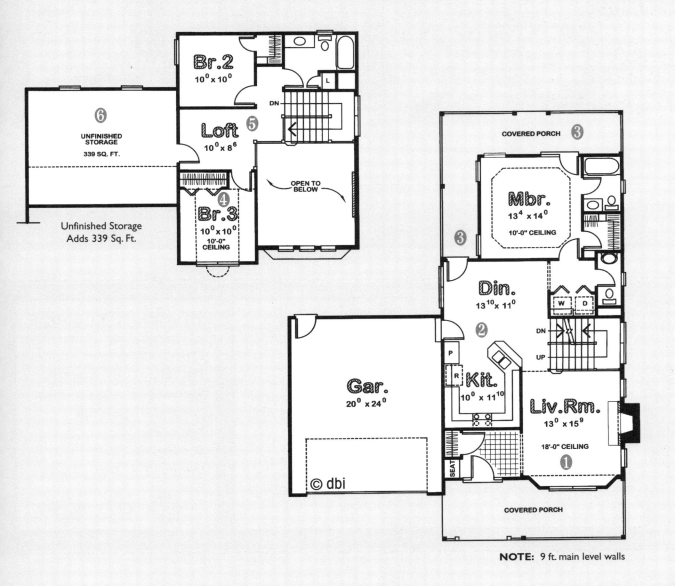

⑥

UNFINISHED STORAGE

339 SQ. FT.

Unfinished Storage
Adds 339 Sq. Ft.

Br. 2
10⁰ x 10⁰

Loft **⑤**
10⁰ x 8⁶

DN

L

④

Br. 3
10⁰ x 10⁰
10'-0" CEILING

OPEN TO BELOW

COVERED PORCH **③**

③

Mbr.
13⁴ x 14⁰
10'-0" CEILING

③

Din.
13¹⁰ x 11⁰

W   D

DN

UP

②

Gar.
20⁰ x 24⁰

P

R

Kit.
10⁰ x 11¹⁰

Liv. Rm.
13⁰ x 15⁹
18'-0" CEILING

①

SEAT

© dbi

COVERED PORCH

NOTE: 9 ft. main level walls

THE SEDONA

① Charismatic details on this facade will welcome you home again and again.

② An interior side-load garage is perfect for a narrow-lot situation.

③ The laundry room offers plenty of counter space to fold clothes and is roomy enough to accommodate entry from the garage.

④ A sloped ceiling adds interesting appeal to the fireplace and windows in the great room.

⑤ The garage easily has room for a work area and shelving for tools.

⑥ Unfinished storage on the second floor could complement the secondary bedrooms as a play area.

PLAN HPT040026

Type: 1½-Story
First Floor: 1,331 square feet
Second Floor: 424 square feet
Total: 1,755 square feet
Bedrooms: 3
Bathrooms: 2½
Width: 52'-0" **Depth:** 59'-4"

MEMORIES . . .

The great room's long, open stairway may cause
Dad to reminisce about a night long ago when he
fidgeted as Grandpa looked him up and down-until
he forgot his nervousness when Mom floated down
the stairs in her baby-blue prom dress.

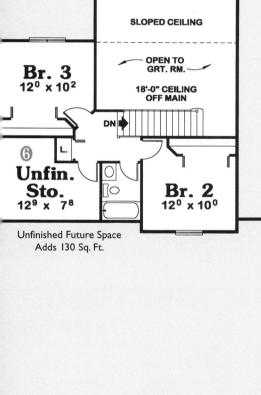

SLOPED CEILING

OPEN TO
GRT. RM.

18'-0" CEILING
OFF MAIN

DN

Br. 3
12⁰ x 10²

⑥
**Unfin.
Sto.**
12⁹ x 7⁸

L.

Br. 2
12⁰ x 10⁰

Unfinished Future Space
Adds 130 Sq. Ft.

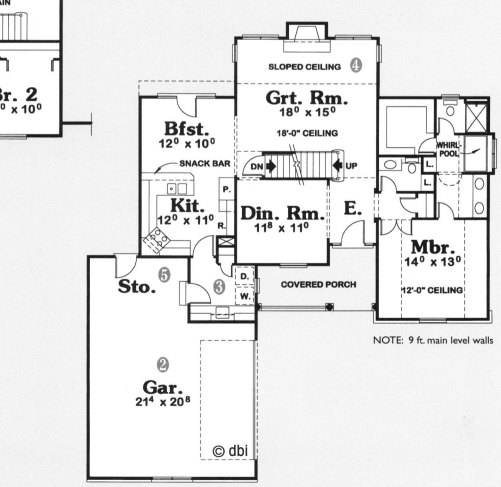

SLOPED CEILING ④

Grt. Rm.
18⁰ x 15⁰

18'-0" CEILING

Bfst.
12⁰ x 10⁰

SNACK BAR

Kit.
12⁰ x 11⁰

P.

R.

DN

UP

WHIRL-
POOL

L.

L.

Din. Rm.
11⁸ x 11⁰

E.

Mbr.
14⁰ x 13⁰

Sto. ⑤

③

D.

W.

COVERED PORCH

12'-0" CEILING

②

Gar.
21⁴ x 20⁸

© dbi

NOTE: 9 ft. main level walls

THE TECOMA

❶ Separated from the second floor, the master suite provides a walk-in closet, whirlpool tub and dual-lav vanity.

❷ Elegant upon entry, the dining room shows off a lovely window to the front.

❸ Patio doors in the breakfast area lead to a natural place for a deck.

❹ Tall windows in the corners of the great room bring in an abundance of light to the volume space.

❺ Informal meals are easily served on the large snack bar in the kitchen.

❻ A large linen closet on the second floor is great for storing toys or games.

PLAN HPT040027

Type: 1½-Story
First Floor: 1,363 square feet
Second Floor: 399 square feet
Total: 1,762 square feet
Bedrooms: 3
Bathrooms: 2½
Width: 55'-0" **Depth:** 46'-4"

MEMORIES . . .

If you were lucky, there was one closet somewhere in the house you grew up in as big as the walk-in closet in this master bedroom. It made the perfect place to hide while playing hide-and-go-seek.

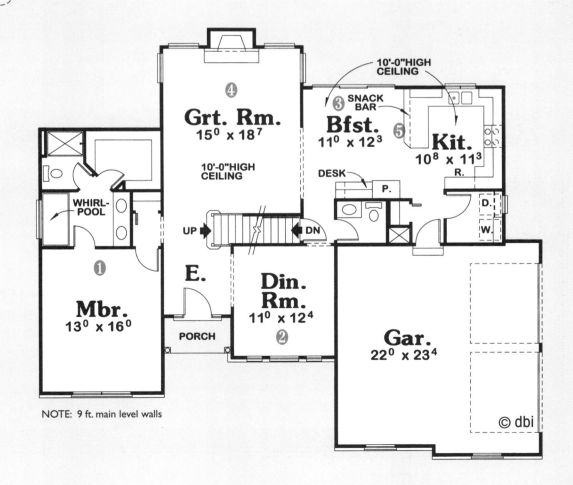

DN

L.

⑥

Br.3
11^0 x 10^0

Br.2
10^4 x 11^0

10'-0"HIGH
CEILING

④

Grt. Rm.
15^0 x 18^7

10'-0"HIGH
CEILING

③ SNACK
BAR

Bfst.
11^0 x 12^3

⑤

Kit.
10^8 x 11^3

R.

DESK

P.

D.

W.

WHIRL-
POOL

UP

DN

①

Mbr.
13^0 x 16^0

E.

**Din.
Rm.**
11^0 x 12^4

②

PORCH

Gar.
22^0 x 23^4

© dbi

NOTE: 9 ft. main level walls

THE MARCELL

 Handsome detailing and unique windows are hallmarks on the front elevation of this design.

 In the entry, a U-shaped staircase with a window leads to a second-floor balcony, two bedrooms and a full bath.

 Triple-arch windows in the front and rear of the great room create an impressive view.

 An island counter in the kitchen is within steps of the stove and sink, making it convenient for preparing meals.

 A compartmented master bath provides a well-planned convenient dressing area with vanity space.

 Spacious secondary bedrooms easily grant room for a desk or toy chest.

PLAN HPT040028

Type: 1½-Story
First Floor: 1,314 square feet
Second Floor: 458 square feet
Total: 1,772 square feet
Bedrooms: 3
Bathrooms: 2½
Width: 52'-0" **Depth:** 51'-4"

MEMORIES . . .

Such a spacious great room summons memories of slumber parties—a misnamed event that was really a marathon of make-overs (or wrestling matches), junk food, ghost stories, giggles and whispers that lasted until dawn.

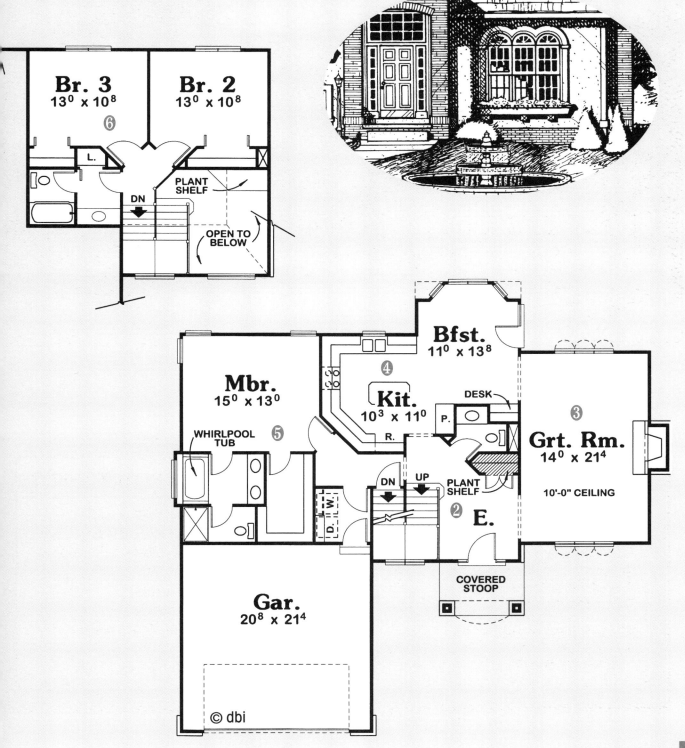

Br. 3
13⁰ x 10⁸

Br. 2
13⁰ x 10⁸

L.

DN

PLANT SHELF

OPEN TO BELOW

Bfst.
11⁰ x 13⁸

Mbr.
15⁰ x 13⁰

WHIRLPOOL TUB

Kit.
10³ x 11⁰

R.

DESK

P.

Grt. Rm.
14⁰ x 21⁴

10'-0" CEILING

D. W.

DN   UP

PLANT SHELF

E.

COVERED STOOP

Gar.
20⁸ x 21⁴

© dbi

THE BRITTANY

① Corner transom-topped windows, an 11-foot ceiling and a lovely fireplace add impact to the great room.

② Interesting angles and a unique snack bar highlight an unforgettable kitchen.

③ A picturesque bowed breakfast area links the kitchen and great room.

④ Master bedroom has 9-foot boxed ceiling, large walk-in closet and pampering bath.

⑤ The powder room is centrally located on the main floor off the breakfast area.

⑥ From the second floor balcony, a view of the entry below provides drama.

PLAN HPT040029

Type: 1½-Story
First Floor: 1,191 square feet
Second Floor: 597 square feet
Total: 1,788 square feet
Bedrooms: 4
Bathrooms: 2½
Width: 50'-0" **Depth:** 48'-0"

MEMORIES . . .

Remember sharing a bedroom with your brother?
The pillow fights, the wrestling matches, the
arguments over who got the top bunk, the time
you divided the room and warned him not to
cross the line? With four bedrooms, everyone
could have had their own room.

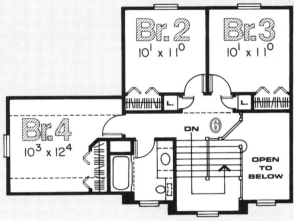

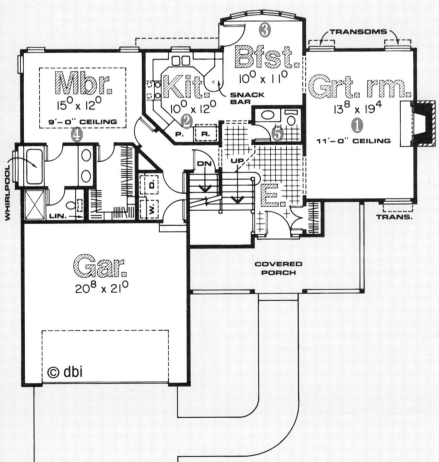

THE KIRKWOOD

① A covered porch with a quaint flower box highlights this home's clean facade.

② Inside, a wide entry leads to a stairway with a vista of the great room from its midway landing.

③ An informal kitchen is uniquely located to the front of the home.

④ The master suite features a dual-sink vanity, whirlpool tub, large walk-in closet and an elegant window to the front.

⑤ Walk-in closets in two secondary bedrooms provide more room for storage.

⑥ An alcove in the garage provides a convenient place for tools and lawn equipment.

PLAN HPT040030

Type: 1½-Story
First Floor: 1,285 square feet
Second Floor: 568 square feet
Total: 1,853 square feet
Bedrooms: 4
Bathrooms: 2½
Width: 59'-8" **Depth:** 42'-8"

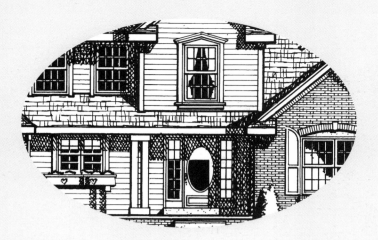

MEMORIES . . .

Who ever forgets their first bike? Whether it was hot pink with streamers in the handles or cobalt blue with ape-hanger handlebars, a banana seat and cards clothes-pinned to the spokes, it was your prize possession. The extra storage space in this garage would have been the perfect place to park it.

SLOPED CEILING

OPEN TO GRT. RM.

16'-5" CEILING

Br. 4
11⁰ × 10⁰

⑤

Br. 3
11⁰ × 10⁰

⑤

Br. 2
11⁰ × 10⁰

DN

Sto.
⑥

Gar.
22⁰ × 20⁸

W. D.

Din.
11⁰ × 11⁴

SNACK BAR

③

Kit.
11⁰ × 12⁰

P. R.

Grt. Rm.
15⁴ × 18⁰

DN

UP

E.

© dbi

COVERED PORCH ❶

④

Mbr.
14⁰ × 14⁰

THE BARONS

❶ The master suite is near the laundry room and features a walk-in closet, soaking tub, separate shower and dual-sink vanity.

❷ Just beyond the entry in this home, a ceiling soars two stories in the family room.

❸ A vaulted ceiling emphasizes the dining room's front window.

❹ Adjoining the kitchen are a butler's pantry and serving counter.

❺ An upper-level attic offers a place for storage within this home.

❻ Two additional bedrooms on the second level share a full bath.

PLAN HPT040031

Type: 1½-Story
First Floor: 1,448 square feet
Second Floor: 449 square feet
Total: 1,897 square feet
Bedrooms: 3
Bathrooms: 2½
Width: 48'-0" **Depth:** 48'-0"

Memories . . .

As kids, the one thing we all had in common was putting our chores off as long as we could—taking out the trash; picking up our room; folding laundry; feeding the dog; washing dishes... Even a kid wouldn't mind doing dishes in this kitchen—with its open view to the family room (and the T.V.).

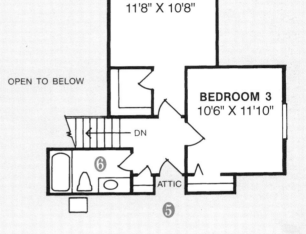

BEDROOM 2
11'8" X 10'8"

OPEN TO BELOW

BEDROOM 3
10'6" X 11'10"

DN

❻

ATTIC

❺

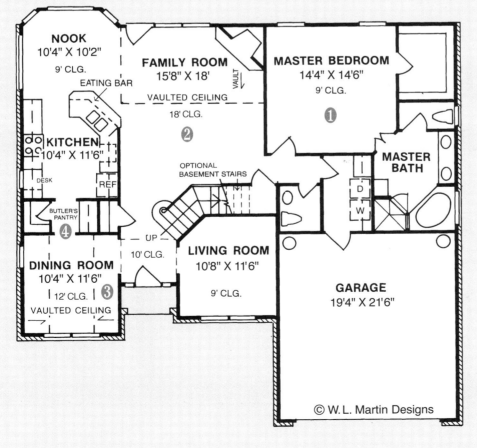

NOOK
10'4" X 10'2"
9' CLG.

EATING BAR

FAMILY ROOM
15'8" X 18'
VAULTED CEILING

18' CLG.

❷

MASTER BEDROOM
14'4" X 14'6"
9' CLG.

❶

VAULT

KITCHEN
10'4" X 11'6"

DESK

REF

OPTIONAL
BASEMENT STAIRS

MASTER
BATH

D
W

BUTLER'S
PANTRY

❹

UP

10' CLG.

LIVING ROOM
10'8" X 11'6"

9' CLG.

GARAGE
19'4" X 21'6"

DINING ROOM
10'4" X 11'6"

12' CLG. ❸

VAULTED CEILING

© W. L. Martin Designs

THE PATERSON

① An inviting front porch welcomes guests

② Spacious great room with volume ceiling, generous windows and see-thru fireplace is open to entry.

③ Hearth kitchen features bayed breakfast area and large planning desk.

④ With a coat closet and laundry sink, the main floor laundry doubles as a mud entry from the garage.

⑤ A sloped ceiling adds elegance to the master suite with a walk-in closet. The pampering bath includes a double vanity and whirlpool tub with window.

⑥ Future expansion is possible over the garage—with access off the hall.

PLAN HPT040032

Type: 1½-Story
First Floor: 1,421 square feet
Second Floor: 578 square feet
Total: 1,999 square feet
Bedrooms: 4
Bathrooms: 2½
Width: 52'-0" **Depth:** 47'-4"

Memories . . .

It wasn't until you grew up that you realized how much your mother did. On top of cooking and cleaning, she stretched the budget, kept everyone organized, soothed broken hearts, mended torn clothes and nursed us when we were sick. A main floor laundry would have made her life easier.

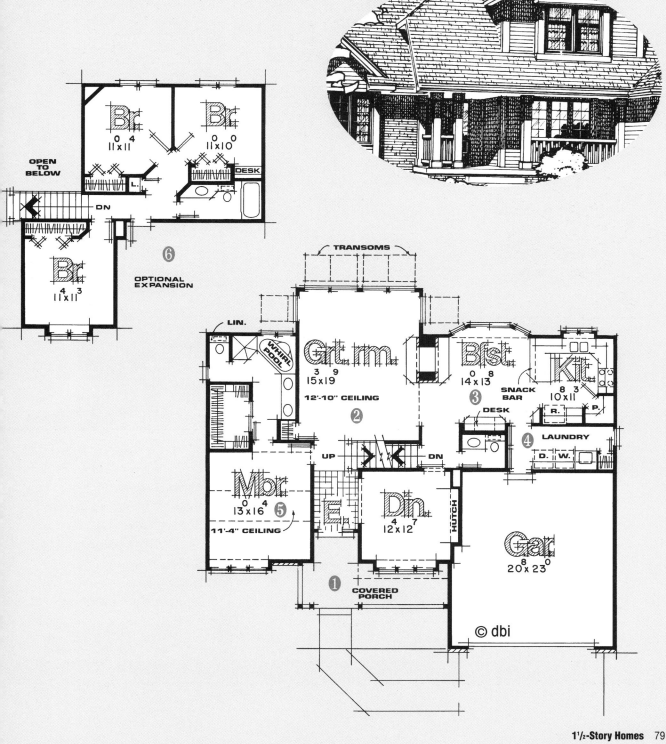

THE SIMONS

① Attractive windows mask this home's side load garage from a view of the street.

② This home's front porch welcomes a swing or pair of chairs for relaxing.

③ A walk-in pantry is ideal for food and appliance storage in the kitchen.

④ A built-in TV cabinet is located next to a fireplace in the living room.

⑤ The master suite features a bayed sitting area and walk-in closet with built-in dresser.

⑥ Guests will enjoy the private bath in bedroom 2 on the upper level.

PLAN HPT040033

Type: 1½-Story
First Floor: 1,383 square feet
Second Floor: 703 square feet
Total: 2,086 square feet
Bedrooms: 4
Bathrooms: 3½
Width: 49'-0" **Depth:** 50'-0"

BEDROOM 2
11'6" X 12'8"

6

DESK

DN

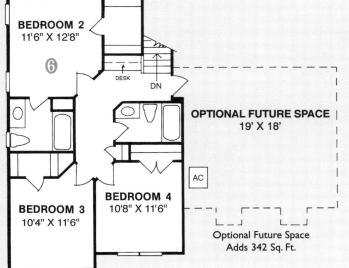

BEDROOM 3
10'4" X 11'6"

BEDROOM 4
10'8" X 11'6"

AC

OPTIONAL FUTURE SPACE
19' X 18'

Optional Future Space
Adds 342 Sq. Ft.

MEMORIES . . .

Sunday dinner with all the relatives—
the grown-ups ate at the big table in the
dining room; the kids gathered in the
kitchen or took a tray out to the porch.
With a dining room, nook and two
porches, this home would be ideal for
big, old-fashioned family gatherings.

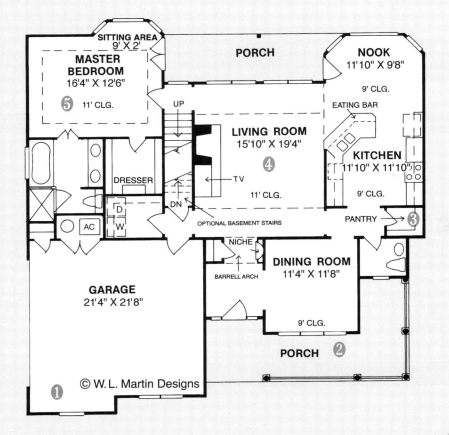

SITTING AREA
9' X 2'

MASTER BEDROOM
16'4" X 12'6"

5 11' CLG.

UP

DRESSER

D
W

AC

PORCH

LIVING ROOM
15'10" X 19'4"

4

TV

11' CLG.

DN

OPTIONAL BASEMENT STAIRS

NOOK
11'10" X 9'8"

9' CLG.

EATING BAR

KITCHEN
11'10" X 11'10"

9' CLG.

PANTRY **3**

NICHE

BARRELL ARCH

DINING ROOM
11'4" X 11'8"

9' CLG.

GARAGE
21'4" X 21'8"

1

© W. L. Martin Designs

PORCH **2**

THE PRAIRIE

❶ An expansive front elevation is enhanced by a covered porch which alludes to a sophisticated interior.

❷ A dramatic entry surveys the dining room with hutch space and great room beyond.

❸ Trapezoid windows and a cathedral ceiling enrich the spacious great room.

❹ The kitchen/breakfast area with nearby laundry and powder bath is designed for convenience and ease.

❺ Secondary bedrooms are secluded on the second level. Bedroom 4 features a volume ceiling and arched window.

❻ On the main floor, the master suite contains a skylit dressing area, corner whirlpool and spacious walk-in closet.

PLAN HPT040034

Type: 1½-Story
First Floor: 1,505 square feet
Second Floor: 610 square feet
Total: 2,115 square feet
Bedrooms: 4
Bathrooms: 2½
Width: 64'-0" **Depth:** 52'-0"

Memories . . .

Your mother had a way of making a house a home—with doilies and dresser scarves, unique knick-knacks, handmade cross-stitched pictures, countless photos of family members and an abundance of houseplants. This breakfast area is sure to be just as homey with plant shelves on two sides.

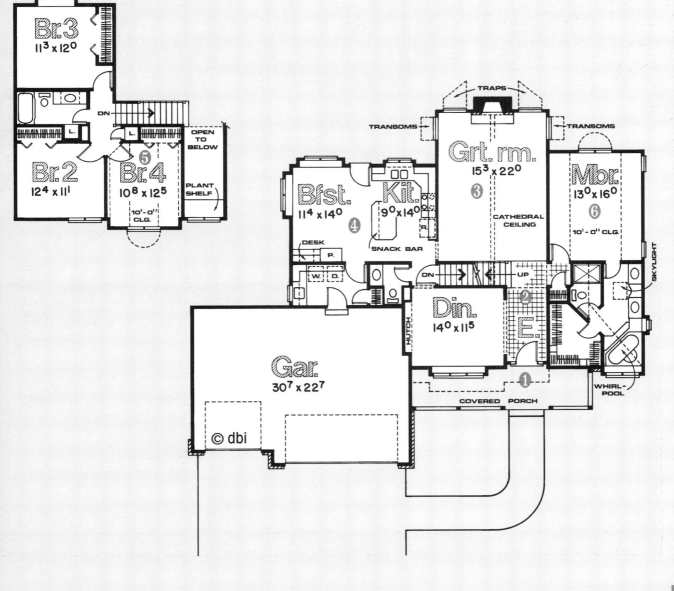

THE BLAIRE

1 A row of three windows capped with shutters draws attention to this home's simple beauty.

2 The practical family area at the rear of the home highlights a large great room that is open to the kitchen and breakfast area.

3 Accompanying the master suite is a large walk-in closet and whirlpool tub across from a dual-lav vanity.

4 A T-shaped stairway makes the second floor accessible from either the front or rear of the home.

5 Bedroom 2 offers a walk-in closet that could be used for storage space.

6 Additional storage space is also offered through an unfinished bonus room above the garage.

PLAN HPT040035

Type: 1½-Story
First Floor: 1,453 square feet
Second Floor: 665 square feet
Total: 2,118 square feet
Bedrooms: 4
Bathrooms: 2½
Width: 55'-0" **Depth:** 49'-0"

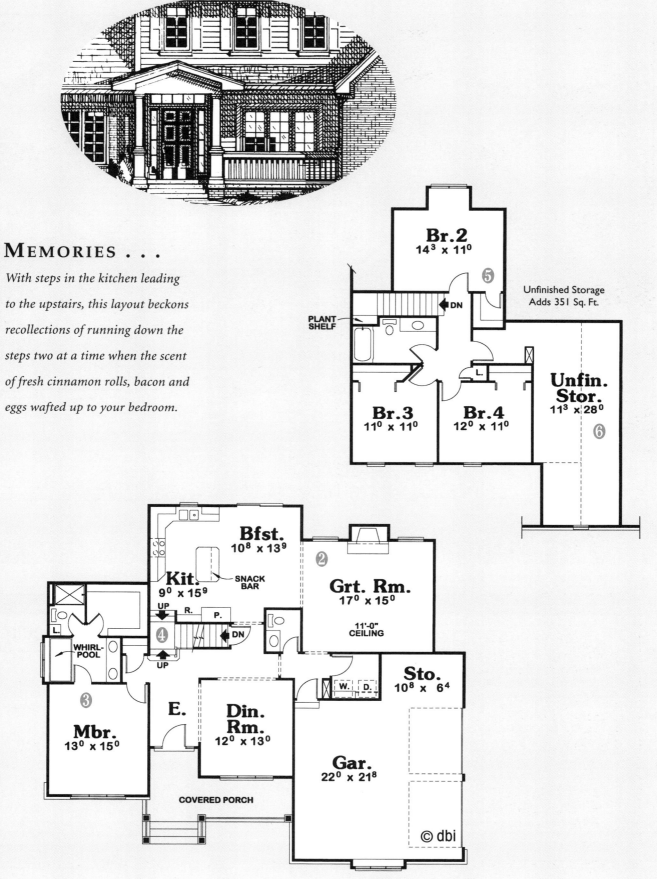

MEMORIES . . .

With steps in the kitchen leading to the upstairs, this layout beckons recollections of running down the steps two at a time when the scent of fresh cinnamon rolls, bacon and eggs wafted up to your bedroom.

Br. 2
14³ x 11⁰

Br. 3
11⁰ x 11⁰

Br. 4
12⁰ x 11⁰

DN

PLANT SHELF

⑤

Unfinished Storage
Adds 351 Sq. Ft.

Unfin. Stor.
11³ x 28⁰

⑥

Bfst.
10⁸ x 13⁹

SNACK BAR

Kit.
9⁰ x 15⁹

UP   R.   P.

DN

④

UP

WHIRL-POOL

③

E.

Mbr.
13⁰ x 15⁰

Din. Rm.
12⁰ x 13⁰

②

Grt. Rm.
17⁰ x 15⁰

11'-0" CEILING

W.   D.

Sto.
10⁸ x 6⁴

Gar.
22⁰ x 21⁸

© dbi

COVERED PORCH

NOTE: 9 ft. main level walls

THE AUBURN

1 This uncomplicated elevation is a welcome sight and coincides with the need to simplify today's lifestyles.

2 The kitchen is strategically located near many living areas, as well as the laundry room and garage.

3 Three second-floor bedrooms will serve relatives for special occasions.

4 An optional home office, hobby room or extra bedroom, the study increases the flexibility of this design.

5 A second, smaller closet in the master suite is perfect for storing seasonal items and clothing.

6 A fireplace and tall windows will add to memorable events in the great room.

PLAN HPT040036

Type: 1½-Story
First Floor: 1,569 square feet
Second Floor: 598 square feet
Total: 2,167 square feet
Bedrooms: 4
Bathrooms: 2½
Width: 55'-8" **Depth:** 52'-4"

MEMORIES . . .

Great Grandma never seemed to care much for television. She preferred to read or listen to the radio. And as she listened, her hands were always busy—crocheting baby booties, knitting afghans, braiding rugs or doing needlework. No doubt she would have really enjoyed this quiet study.

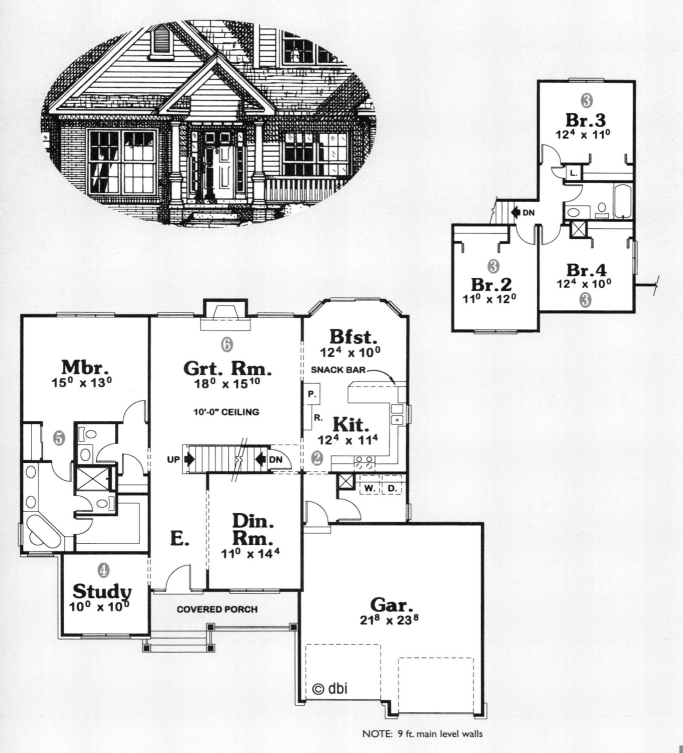

③
Br.3
12⁴ x 11⁰

L.

DN

③
Br.2
11⁰ x 12⁰

Br.4
12⁴ x 10⁰
③

Mbr.
15⁰ x 13⁰

⑥
Grt. Rm.
18⁰ x 15¹⁰

10'-0" CEILING

Bfst.
12⁴ x 10⁰

SNACK BAR

P.

R.

Kit.
12⁴ x 11⁴

UP   DN

②

⑤

W.   D.

Din. Rm.
11⁰ x 14⁴

E.

④
Study
10⁰ x 10⁰

COVERED PORCH

Gar.
21⁸ x 23⁸

© dbi

NOTE: 9 ft. main level walls

THE CAMROSE

❶ Triple-wide windows illuminate both the exterior and interior of this home.

❷ Built-in bookshelves add to the practicality of studying and working in the library.

❸ Bayed windows in the breakfast area provide a beautiful frame for viewing the back.

❹ When family comes to visit, three bedrooms are located on the second floor.

❺ A spacious master suite tempts one to relax in its corner whirlpool tub.

❻ The garage provides a place for storing lawn and garden equipment.

PLAN HPT040037

Type: 1½-Story
First Floor: 1,624 square feet
Second Floor: 566 square feet
Total: 2,190 square feet
Bedrooms: 4
Bathrooms: 2½
Width: 55'-8" **Depth:** 52'-0"

MEMORIES . . .

When you were young, favorite reading materials included Winnie the Pooh, Curious George and Dr. Seuss. As you got older, you probably collected Nancy Drew or Hardy Boys books—until you ran out of room. Wouldn't it have been great to have a house with a library and walls lined with bookshelves?

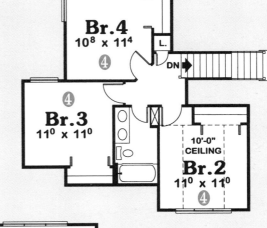

Br.4
10^8 x 11^4
④

Br.3
11^0 x 11^0
④

10'-0"
CEILING
Br.2
11^0 x 11^0
④

DN ▶

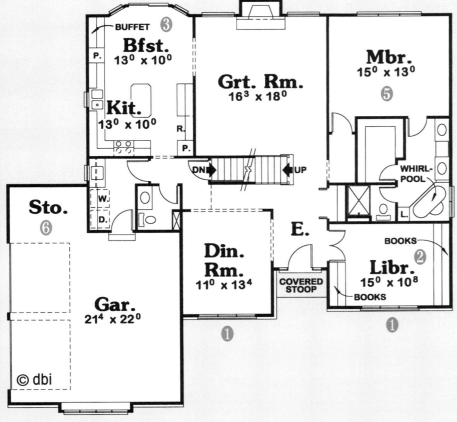

BUFFET ③

P.

Bfst.
13^0 x 10^0

Kit.
13^0 x 10^0

R.

P.

Grt. Rm.
16^3 x 18^0

Mbr.
15^0 x 13^0
⑤

WHIRL-POOL

L.

DN ▶ ◀ UP

Sto.
⑥

W.
D.

E.

Din.
Rm.
11^0 x 13^4

COVERED STOOP

BOOKS

Libr.
15^0 x 10^8
②

BOOKS

Gar.
21^4 x 22^0

© dbi

①   ①

NOTE: 9 ft. main level walls

THE BARDEL

1 A shed roof and vertical siding give this home its cottage feel.

2 A walk-in pantry and butler's pantry conveniently adjoin a spacious dining room with vaulted ceiling.

3 In the kitchen, an angled snack bar connects the family room and breakfast nook.

4 A large walk-in closet, twin-sink vanity and corner garden tub make the master suite a luxurious retreat.

5 All three second floor bedrooms include walk-in closets.

6 Attic space off the bath offers the option of adding storage on the second level.

PLAN HPT040038

Type: 1½-Story
First Floor: 1,568 square feet
Second Floor: 680 square feet
Total: 2,248 square feet
Bedrooms: 4
Bathrooms: 2½
Width: 50'-0" **Depth:** 48'-0"

Memories . . .

When you were young, you probably took your mother's cooking for granted.

As you got older you noticed that no one else's meat loaf, chicken soup, or

spaghetti sauce tasted quite like hers. Imagine how she would have enjoyed

this deluxe kitchen—complete with desk and two pantries.

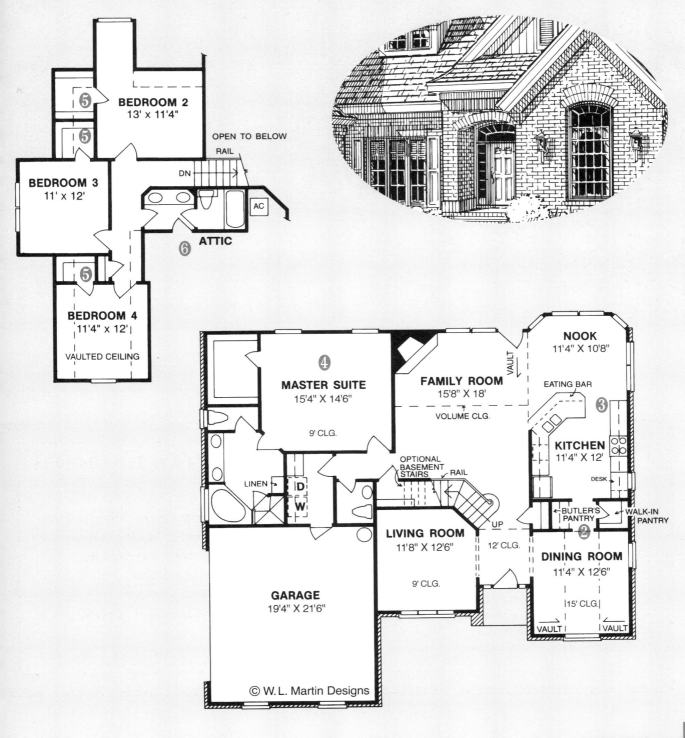

BEDROOM 2
13' x 11'4"

OPEN TO BELOW

RAIL

BEDROOM 3
11' x 12'

DN

AC

⑥ ATTIC

BEDROOM 4
11'4" x 12'

VAULTED CEILING

④ MASTER SUITE
15'4" X 14'6"

9' CLG.

FAMILY ROOM
15'8" X 18'

VAULT

NOOK
11'4" X 10'8"

EATING BAR

③

VOLUME CLG.

KITCHEN
11'4" X 12'

DESK

LINEN

D
W

OPTIONAL
BASEMENT
STAIRS

RAIL

BUTLER'S
PANTRY

WALK-IN
PANTRY

LIVING ROOM
11'8" X 12'6"

9' CLG.

UP

12' CLG.

②

DINING ROOM
11'4" X 12'6"

GARAGE
19'4" X 21'6"

15' CLG.

VAULT

VAULT

© W.L. Martin Designs

THE BOWDEN

1 Brackets and the absence of railing bring an open-air quality to this front porch.

2 Privately located, the study is a great place for a home-based business.

3 Double doors open to the master suite with a bath featuring a large walk-in closet, corner whirlpool tub and separate shower.

4 The dinette and kitchen function together for day-to-day use and offer a planning desk and island counter.

5 Within steps of the kitchen, the dining room extends this home's livability.

6 Unfinished storage on the second floor offers options for expanding living and sleeping areas.

PLAN HPT040039

Type: 1½-Story
First Floor: 1,665 square feet
Second Floor: 674 square feet
Total: 2,339 square feet
Bedrooms: 4
Bathrooms: 2½
Width: 54'-0" **Depth:** 45'-4"

MEMORIES . . .

As youngsters, we found security in routine. The way Mother allocated different days of the week for laundry, baking, housecleaning and grocery shopping. On grocery day, everyone helped carry the sacks in. A door from the garage to the kitchen will make quick work of unloading the trunk.

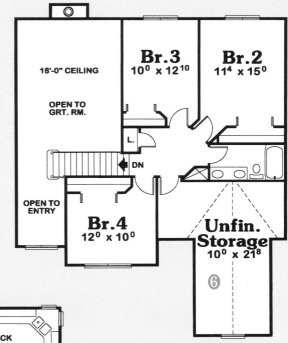

18'-0" CEILING

OPEN TO GRT. RM.

OPEN TO ENTRY

Br.3
10⁰ x 12¹⁰

Br.2
11⁴ x 15⁰

L.

DN

Br.4
12⁰ x 10⁰

Unfin. Storage
10⁰ x 21⁸

⑥

Unfinished Future Space
Adds 293 Sq. Ft.

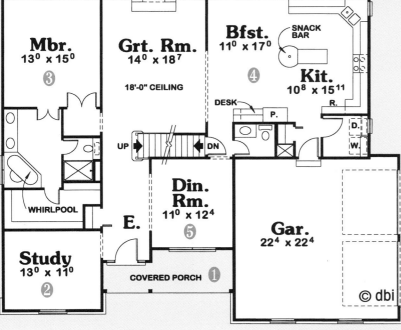

Mbr.
13⁰ x 15⁰

③

Grt. Rm.
14⁰ x 18⁷

18'-0" CEILING

UP   DN

Bfst.
11⁰ x 17⁰

SNACK BAR

④

Kit.
10⁸ x 15¹¹

DESK   P.

R.

D.

W.

WHIRLPOOL

E.

Din. Rm.
11⁰ x 12⁴

⑤

Gar.
22⁴ x 22⁴

Study
13⁰ x 11⁰

②

COVERED PORCH ①

© dbi

NOTE: 9 ft. main level walls

THE KENNETH

❶ The cozy mix of cobblestone and shake siding of this home brings to life the romance of an era long past.

❷ A valley cathedral ceiling and stunning windows highlight the great room.

❸ The large kitchen features an island counter with a snack bar and quick access to a rear stairway.

❹ Located at the top of the stairwell, a loft with bookshelves makes the perfect place for reading or studying, or even a unique fourth bedroom.

❺ An immense walk-in closet with a built-in dresser, whirlpool tub and dual-sink vanity are enclosed behind French doors adding intimacy to the master suite.

PLAN HPT040040

Type: 1½-Story
First Floor: 1,640 square feet
Second Floor: 711 square feet
Total: 2,351 square feet
Bedrooms: 3
Bathrooms: 2½
Width: 51'-4" **Depth:** 54'-0"

MEMORIES . . .

Our siblings: the secrets we shared, the jokes we played on each other and the battles we waged over insignificant things. They were always there through thick and thin and when it came right down to it—the very best of friends. What better place for the kids to hang out together than this loft?

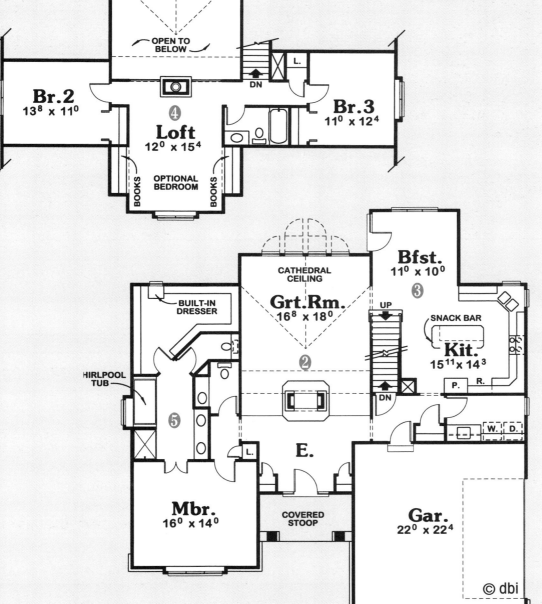

CATHEDRAL CEILING

OPEN TO BELOW

Br.2
13⁸ x 11⁰

④

Loft
12⁰ x 15⁴

DN

L.

Br.3
11⁰ x 12⁴

OPTIONAL BEDROOM

BOOKS

BOOKS

CATHEDRAL CEILING

Bfst.
11⁰ x 10⁰

③

Grt.Rm.
16⁸ x 18⁰

UP

SNACK BAR

②

Kit.
15¹¹ x 14³

BUILT-IN DRESSER

HIRLPOOL TUB

⑤

DN

P.

R.

W.

D.

Mbr.
16⁰ x 14⁰

E.

COVERED STOOP

Gar.
22⁰ x 22⁴

© dbi

NOTE: 9 ft. main level walls

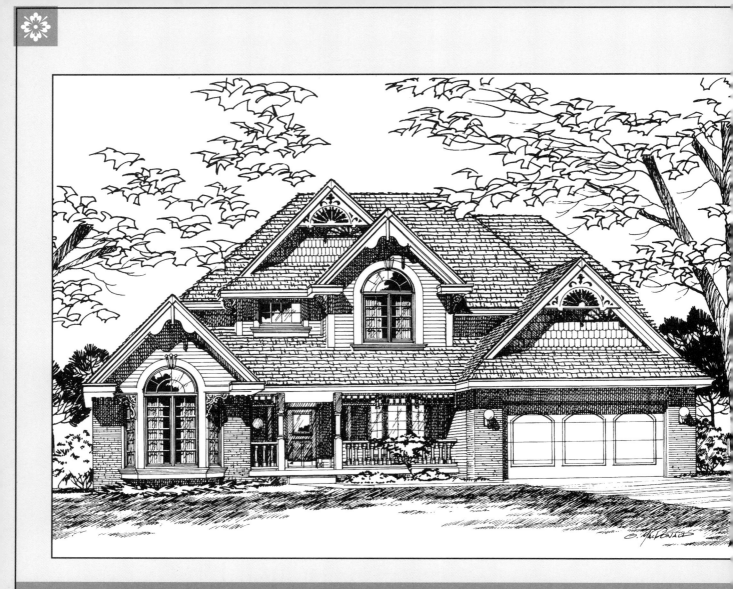

THE MANCHESTER

① Two-story entry showcases the stairway and a formal dining room with attractive bayed window.

② Special details in the great room include a beamed ceiling, see-thru fireplace, built-in bookcase and ample windows.

③ Open kitchen, hearth and breakfast area features bayed dining with arched window, built-in desk and walk-in pantry.

④ The second level offers interesting sill detail on the landing and a plant shelf overlooking area below.

⑤ Comfortable secondary bedrooms share compartmented bath with separate lavs and a clothes chute.

⑥ A main level master suite has arched window, special ceiling, dual lavs, whirlpool tub and two closets.

PLAN HPT040042

Type: 1½-Story
First Floor: 1,653 square feet
Second Floor: 700 square feet
Total: 2,353 square feet
Bedrooms: 4
Bathrooms: 2½
Width: 54'-0" **Depth:** 50'-0"

MEMORIES . . .

Until we were old enough to lend a hand, outdoor chores fell to Dad. Grilling steaks and burgers, mowing the lawn, trimming the bushes, raking leaves, stringing Christmas lights and shoveling snow. The extra storage space in this garage would have been an ideal place to store his tools and supplies.

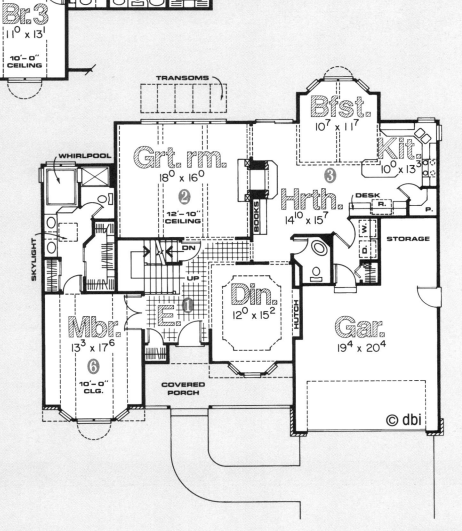

Br. 4
11^2 x 10^0

Br. 2
11^0 x 13^6

DN

CLOTHES CHUTE

⑤

④

OPEN TO BELOW

PLANT SHELF

TRANS.

Br. 3
11^0 x 13^1

10'-0" CEILING

TRANSOMS

WHIRLPOOL

Grt. rm.
18^0 x 16^0

②

12'-10" CEILING

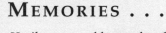
Bfst.
10^7 x 11^7

Kit.
10^0 x 13^3

③

Hrth.
14^{10} x 15^7

DESK

R.

P.

BOOKS

SKYLIGHT

DN

UP

STORAGE

D.

W.

Din.
12^0 x 15^2

HUTCH

Gar.
19^4 x 20^4

Mbr.
13^3 x 17^6

⑥

10'-0" CLG.

①

COVERED PORCH

© dbi

DESIGNERS' INK

THE MAGRATH

①A classic Greek-style entry brings structure to this asymmetrical design.

②A study located on the second floor is perfect as a homework area.

③Angled walls and a 10-foot ceiling define the dining room and establish its pleasant ambiance.

④A hall leads to a private master suite with a large sitting room, great for relaxing or catching up on office work.

⑤Quaint window seats charm bedrooms 2 and 3.

⑥A large bonus room above the garage is beneficial for seasonal storage.

PLAN HPT040043

Type: 1½-Story
First Floor: 1,554 square feet
Second Floor: 867 square feet
Total: 2,421 square feet
Bedrooms: 4
Bathrooms: 2½
Width: 47'-8" **Depth:** 52'-4"

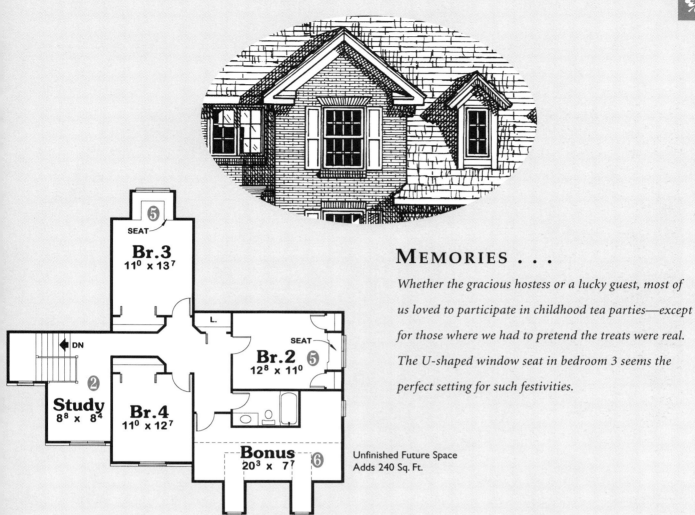

Memories . . .

Whether the gracious hostess or a lucky guest, most of us loved to participate in childhood tea parties—except for those where we had to pretend the treats were real. The U-shaped window seat in bedroom 3 seems the perfect setting for such festivities.

Br.3
11^0 x 13^7

SEAT

⑤

⑤

DN

Br.2
12^8 x 11^0

SEAT

②

Study
8^8 x 8^4

Br.4
11^0 x 12^7

L.

Bonus
20^3 x 7^7

⑥

Unfinished Future Space
Adds 240 Sq. Ft.

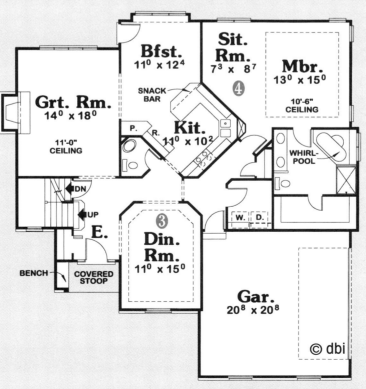

Bfst.
11^0 x 12^4

**Sit.
Rm.**
7^3 x 8^7

④

Mbr.
13^0 x 15^0

10'-6"
CEILING

Grt. Rm.
14^0 x 18^0

11'-0"
CEILING

SNACK
BAR

P.   R.

Kit.
11^0 x 10^2

WHIRL-
POOL

DN

UP

E.

③

**Din.
Rm.**
11^0 x 15^0

W.   D.

BENCH

COVERED
STOOP

Gar.
20^8 x 20^8

© dbi

NOTE: 9 ft. main level walls

THE FAIRMONT

① The formal living and dining room line the foyer and create an immediate impression of elegance upon entering this home.

② A built-in bookcase can be enjoyed by those in the master suite or great room.

③ His and her vanities are convenient in the master bath and flank an oval whirlpool tub.

④ Both a hanging closet and a soaking sink offer further functionality to the main floor laundry room.

⑤ Spacious secondary bedrooms will easily accommodate a toy chest or a desk.

⑥ In the garage, a convenient alcove is a perfect area to install storage shelves.

PLAN HPT040044

Type: 1½-Story
First Floor: 1,755 square feet
Second Floor: 693 square feet
Total: 2,448 square feet
Bedrooms: 4
Bathrooms: 2½
Width: 62'-0" **Depth:** 44'-4"

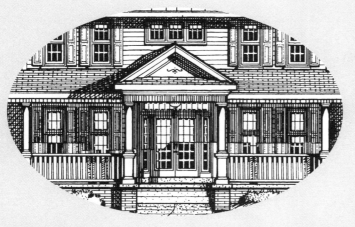

MEMORIES . . .

It's easy to imagine a swing hanging from the corner of this wrap-around porch. It's also easy to see images of the past: reading stories to your dolls, playing jacks with your buddies, sitting on the rail watching your big brother do wheelies on his bike, sitting on the swing with your first date.

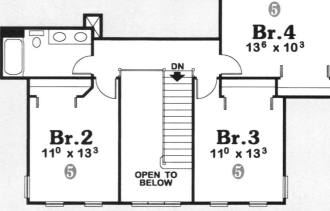

Br.4
13⁶ x 10³

Br.2
11⁰ x 13³

DN

OPEN TO BELOW

Br.3
11⁰ x 13³

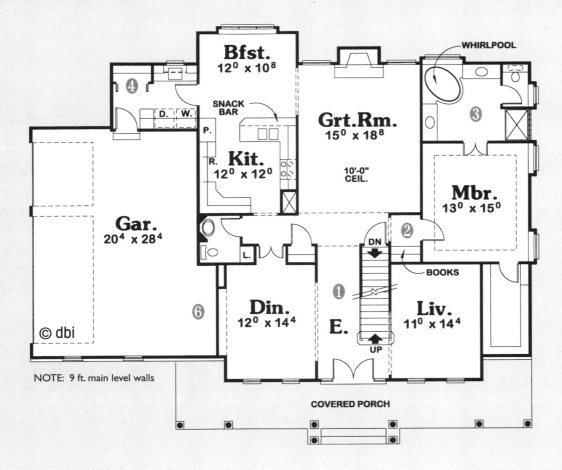

Bfst.
12⁰ x 10⁸

WHIRLPOOL

SNACK BAR

D. W.

P.

R.

Kit.
12⁰ x 12⁰

Grt.Rm.
15⁰ x 18⁸

10'-0" CEIL.

Mbr.
13⁰ x 15⁰

Gar.
20⁴ x 28⁴

L.

DN

BOOKS

© dbi

Din.
12⁰ x 14⁴

E.

UP

Liv.
11⁰ x 14⁴

NOTE: 9 ft. main level walls

COVERED PORCH

THE CAREY

① The two-story entry radiates light into the home with a distinctive dormer.

② Special hutch space was designed into the elegant bayed dining room.

③ Double doors reveal the master suite with his and her walk-in closets and a 10-foot vaulted ceiling.

④ Built-in bookshelves and a fireplace will invite leisure in the hearth room.

⑤ Showcased just off the breakfast area, a walk-in pantry and island counter benefit the kitchen.

⑥ The stairway features an open railing and balcony that's visible from the great room.

PLAN HPT040045

Type: 1½-Story
First Floor: 1,795 square feet
Second Floor: 717 square feet
Total: 2,512 square feet
Bedrooms: 4
Bathrooms: 2½
Width: 57'-0" **Depth:** 51'-0"

MEMORIES . . .

The built-in desk in this kitchen reminds one of countless evenings working on homework at the kitchen table while Mom prepared supper, explained difficult math problems, quizzed you on your spelling words and listened to your book report.

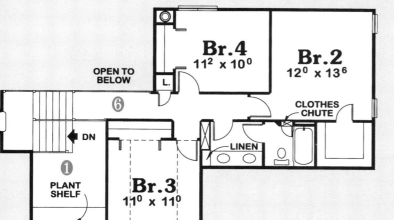

OPEN TO BELOW

Br.4
11^2 x 10^0

Br.2
12^0 x 13^6

CLOTHES CHUTE

❻

DN

❶

PLANT SHELF

LINEN

Br.3
11^0 x 11^0

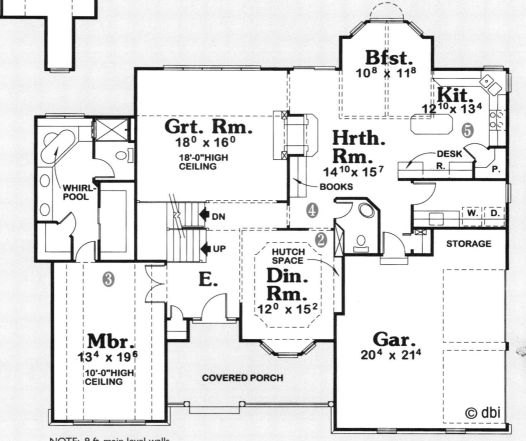

Bfst.
10^8 x 11^8

Kit.
12^{10} x 13^4

Grt. Rm.
18^0 x 16^0
18'-0" HIGH CEILING

Hrth. Rm.
14^{10} x 15^7

BOOKS

❺

DESK

R.

P.

WHIRL-POOL

DN

❹

UP

❷

W. **D.**

STORAGE

❸

E.

HUTCH SPACE

Din. Rm.
12^0 x 15^2

Mbr.
13^4 x 19^6
10'-0" HIGH CEILING

COVERED PORCH

Gar.
20^4 x 21^4

© dbi

NOTE: 9 ft. main level walls

THE HANNA

① The discreet Prairie-style influence of this facade will be celebrated wherever it is built.

② A see-thru fireplace adds a sense of rugged warmth to the kitchen while making an elegant showpiece in the great room.

③ Midway up the staircase, double doors lead to the master suite with built-in bookcases, his and her walk-in closets, a barrel-vault ceiling and oval whirlpool tub.

④ On the second floor, a computer loft with a built-in desk overlooks the impressive great room.

⑤ Bedroom 2 has bookshelves on either side of a triple-wide window and could easily be converted to a study.

PLAN HPT040046

Type: 1½-Story
First Floor: 1,735 square feet
Second Floor: 841 square feet
Total: 2,576 square feet
Bedrooms: 4
Bathrooms: 2½
Width: 58'-8" **Depth:** 54'-0"

MEMORIES . . .

Like most kids, you probably had a collection of special treasures.... an autographed base-ball, model airplanes and soccer trophies—or 4-H ribbons, Barbie dolls and clay sculptures you made in art class. Wouldn't it have been great to have built-in shelves like those in bedroom 2 where you could display them?

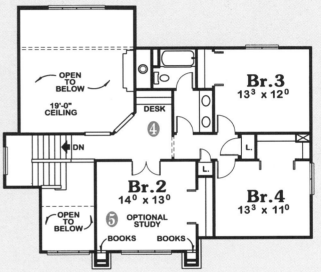

OPEN TO BELOW

19'-0" CEILING

DESK

④

Br.3
13³ x 12⁰

DN

OPEN TO BELOW

Br.2
14⁰ x 13⁰

⑤ OPTIONAL STUDY

BOOKS   BOOKS

Br.4
13³ x 11⁰

L.

L.

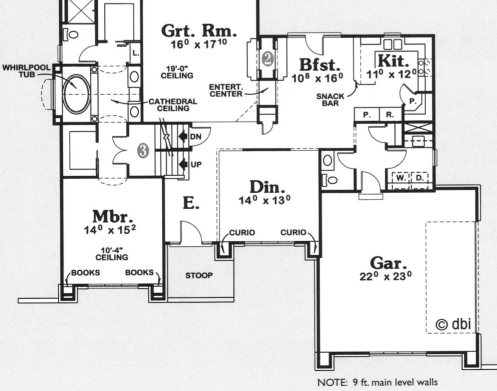

WHIRLPOOL TUB

Grt. Rm.
16⁰ x 17¹⁰

19'-0" CEILING

②

ENTERT. CENTER

CATHEDRAL CEILING

Bfst.
10⁸ x 16⁰

SNACK BAR

Kit.
11⁰ x 12⁰

P.   R.

③   DN

UP

L.

Mbr.
14⁰ x 15²

10'-4" CEILING

BOOKS   BOOKS

E.

STOOP

CURIO   CURIO

Din.
14⁰ x 13⁰

W. D.

P.

Gar.
22⁰ x 23⁰

© dbi

NOTE: 9 ft. main level walls

THE SCHUYLER

1 Timeless details in unique proportions give this design its eclectic design.

2 When entertaining, the den with double doors makes a wonderful companion to the dining room.

3 Bayed windows brighten the breakfast area which is open to the kitchen with a peninsula snack bar.

4 Adding glamour to the entry, the dining room features a hutch space.

5 Eleven-foot-high ceilings in the master bedroom and great room bring a sense of openness to daily living.

6 An unfinished storage space offers the potential for a hobby room or exercise area.

PLAN HPT040047

Type: 1½-Story
First Floor: 1,847 square feet
Second Floor: 766 square feet
Total: 2,613 square feet
Bedrooms: 4
Bathrooms: 2½
Width: 60'-0" **Depth:** 59'-4"

Memories . . .

A door from the garage leading to the kitchen no doubt reminds you of bursting through the door yelling: "What's for supper, Mom?" Of course there were days when an unmistakable aroma told you there was a pot of spaghetti on the stove, a roast baking in the oven or chicken sizzling in the frying pan.

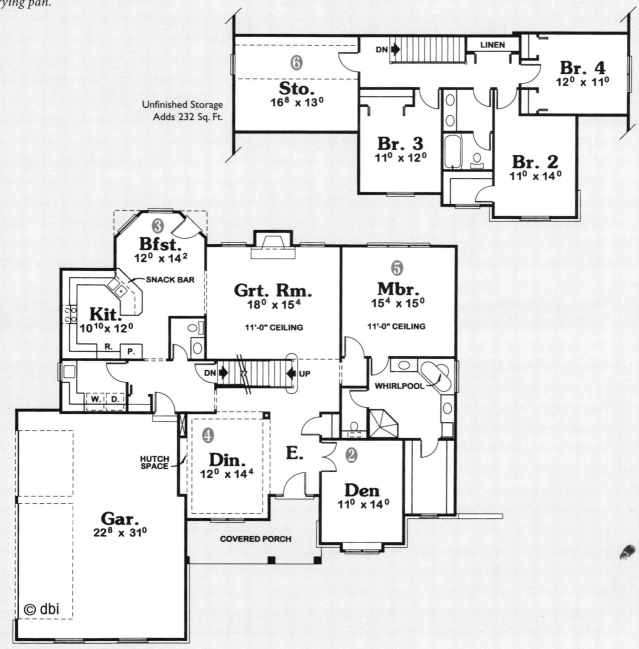

⑥ Sto.
16^8 x 13^0

DN   LINEN

Br. 4
12^0 x 11^0

Unfinished Storage
Adds 232 Sq. Ft.

Br. 3
11^0 x 12^0

Br. 2
11^0 x 14^0

③ Bfst.
12^0 x 14^2

SNACK BAR

Kit.
10^{10} x 12^0

R.   P.

Grt. Rm.
18^0 x 15^4
11'-0" CEILING

⑤ Mbr.
15^4 x 15^0
11'-0" CEILING

DN   UP

WHIRLPOOL

W.   D.

HUTCH
SPACE

④ Din.
12^0 x 14^4

E.

② Den
11^0 x 14^0

Gar.
22^8 x 31^0

© dbi

COVERED PORCH

NOTE: 9 ft. main level walls

THE PHILIPSBURG

① The mid-level landing on the stairway overlooks the two-story great room with see-thru fireplace.

② Built-in cabinetry in the hearth room will be convenient whether watching television in the morning or evening.

③ A walk-in pantry and island counter help create an organized atmosphere in the kitchen.

④ A rear covered porch located off the breakfast area is a great place to relax.

⑤ His and her walk-in closets, a double vanity and whirlpool tub pamper the master suite.

⑥ Built-in bookshelves and an arched entry bring distinction to a sitting room off the master suite.

PLAN HPT040048

Type: 1½-Story
First Floor: 1,955 square feet
Second Floor: 660 square feet
Total: 2,615 square feet
Bedrooms: 4
Bathrooms: 2½
Width: 60'-0" **Depth:** 60'-4"

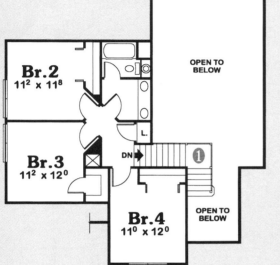

Br.2
11^2 x 11^8

Br.3
11^2 x 12^0

Br.4
11^0 x 12^0

OPEN TO BELOW

OPEN TO BELOW

DN ➤

1

L.

MEMORIES . . .

One of the things that makes us remember the good old days so fondly was the way life moved at a slower pace. With today's hectic lifestyles, the secret to contentment is taking the time to relax the way we did then—sitting on a rocker on the front porch sipping a tall glass of lemonade.

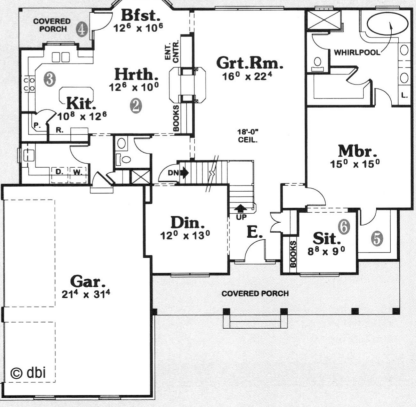

COVERED PORCH **4**

Bfst.
12^6 x 10^6

3

Hrth.
12^6 x 10^0

Kit.
10^8 x 12^6

2

P. R.

D. W.

ENT. CNTR.

BOOKS

Grt.Rm.
16^0 x 22^4

18'-0" CEIL.

WHIRLPOOL

L.

Mbr.
15^0 x 15^0

DN ➤

Din.
12^0 x 13^0

UP

E.

BOOKS

Sit.
8^8 x 9^0

6

5

Gar.
21^4 x 31^4

© dbi

COVERED PORCH

NOTE: 9 ft. main level walls

THE ROWENA

❶ This pleasant elevation offers a warm welcome through elements such as its front porch and use of siding and brick.

❷ Formal rooms polish the entry and offer views past the front porch.

❸ Triple windows and a built-in bookshelf add luster to the master bedroom.

❹ Three sides of windows bring a cheerful atmosphere to the breakfast area, as well as the kitchen.

❺ All three second floor bedrooms features walk-in closets.

❻ Unfinished storage on the second floor is beneficial for keeping seasonal items or storing kids' items while away at college.

PLAN HPT040049

Type: 1¹/₂-Story
First Floor: 1,870 square feet
Second Floor: 767 square feet
Total: 2,637 square feet
Bedrooms: 4
Bathrooms: 2¹/₂
Width: 59'-4" **Depth:** 61'-4"

MEMORIES . . .

Life seemed to revolve around music during your teen years. You spent your free time in your room listening to records, teaching yourself to play guitar and reading magazines about your favorite singers. With extra space for an easy chair, bedroom 3 would have been an ideal set-up.

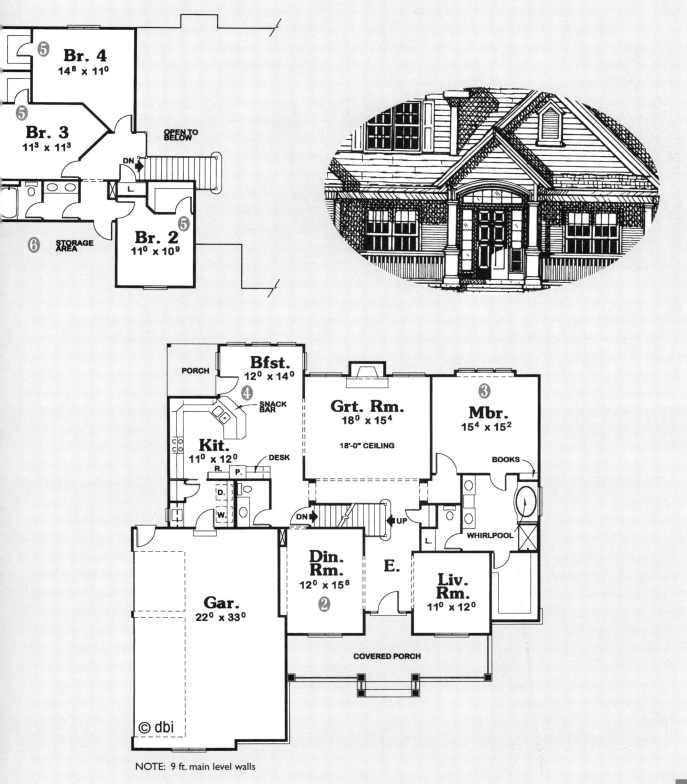

⑤ **Br. 4**
14⁸ x 11⁰

⑤ **Br. 3**
11³ x 11³

OPEN TO BELOW

DN

L.

⑥ STORAGE AREA

⑤ **Br. 2**
11⁰ x 10⁹

PORCH

Bfst.
12⁰ x 14⁰

④ SNACK BAR

Grt. Rm.
18⁰ x 15⁴

18'-0" CEILING

③ **Mbr.**
15⁴ x 15²

BOOKS

Kit.
11⁰ x 12⁰

DESK

R. P.

D.

W.

DN

UP

L.

WHIRLPOOL

Gar.
22⁰ x 33⁰

Din. Rm.
12⁰ x 15⁸

② E.

Liv. Rm.
11⁰ x 12⁰

COVERED PORCH

© dbi

NOTE: 9 ft. main level walls

THE WILKS MANOR

❶ This elevation offers a variety of pleasing details—a tall chimney, bayed wrought-iron widow's balcony and triple windows set under a hip roof.

❷ Windows on two walls bring light into a winding staircase that leads to the second level.

❸ A spacious guest suite enjoys privacy in a secluded wing.

❹ A huge kitchen features an angled snack bar, pantry and lengthy expanse of cabinets and counters.

❺ Cathedral ceilings extend through the family room to the covered porch in the back of the home.

❻ In the master bedroom and bath, cathedral ceilings increase the feeling of spaciousness.

PLAN HPT040050

Type: 1½-Story
First Floor: 2,087 square feet
Second Floor: 552 square feet
Total: 2,639 square feet
Bedrooms: 3
Bathrooms: 3½
Width: 68'-7" **Depth:** 57'-4"

MEMORIES . . .

Grandma's visits were priceless times. The surprise she always brought along in her suitcase. The endless hugs. The way she listened to you as if you were the most fascinating person in the world. Maybe she would have stayed a little longer with a guest room like this.

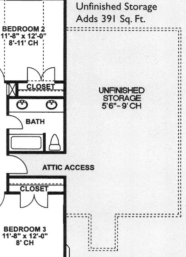

Unfinished Storage Adds 391 Sq. Ft.

BEDROOM 2
11'-8" x 12'-0"
8'-11' CH

CLOSET

UNFINISHED STORAGE
5'6" - 9' CH

FAMILY ROOM BELOW
CATHEDRAL CLG.

BATH

ATTIC ACCESS

2-STORY ENTRY
18' CH

CLOSET

BEDROOM 3
11'-8" x 12'-0"
8' CH

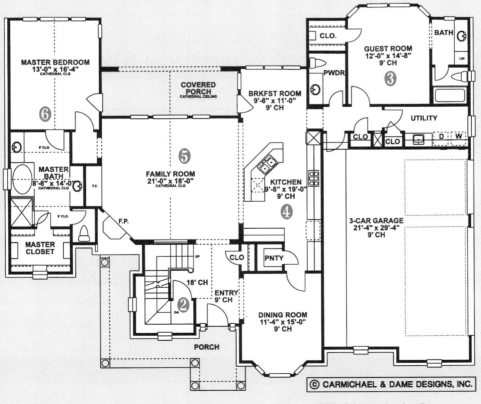

MASTER BEDROOM
13'-0" x 16'-4"
CATHEDRAL CLG

⑥

COVERED PORCH
CATHEDRAL CEILING

CLO.

GUEST ROOM
12'-0" x 14'-8"
9' CH

③

BATH

BRKFST ROOM
9'-8" x 11'-0"
9' CH

PWDR

MASTER BATH
8'-8" x 14'-0"
CATHEDRAL CLG

9' CLO.

T.V.

FAMILY ROOM
21'-0" x 18'-0"
CATHEDRAL CLG

⑤

KITCHEN
9'-8" x 19'-0"
9' CH

④

UTILITY

CLO   CLO   D   W

MASTER CLOSET

F.P.

CLO   PNTY

3-CAR GARAGE
21'-4" x 29'-4"
9' CH

②

18' CH

ENTRY
9' CH

DINING ROOM
11'-4" x 15'-0"
9' CH

PORCH

© CARMICHAEL & DAME DESIGNS, INC.

NOTE: 9 ft. main level walls

THE WOODLANDS SHOWCASE

❶ An arched porch leads to an impressive entry with an 18-foot-high ceiling.

❷ Windows in the back of the family room look out onto a covered porch—accessed from the master bedroom and the breakfast area.

❸ Both the study and bedroom 3 enjoy an attractive gazebo shape.

❹ A lofty cathedral ceiling ties the family room and kitchen together.

❺ The second floor balcony enjoys magnificent views into the entry and family room.

❻ A walk-in pantry and a butler's pantry are both conveniently located off the kitchen.

PLAN HPT040051

Type: 1½-Story
First Floor: 1,906 square feet
Second Floor: 749 square feet
Total: 2,655 square feet
Bedrooms: 4
Bathrooms: 2½
Width: 65'-3" **Depth:** 57'-1½"

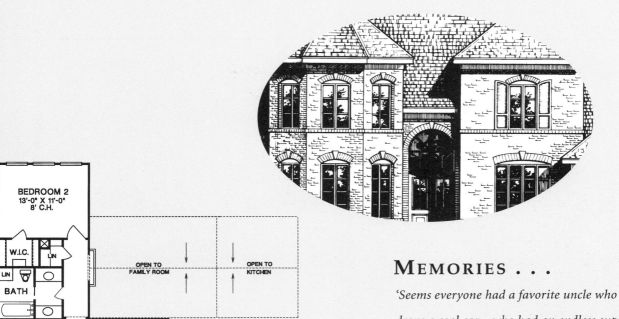

Upper Floor

BEDROOM 2
13'-0" X 11'-0"
8' C.H.

W.I.C.

LIN

LIN

BATH

DN

BALCONY ⑤

ATTIC

OPEN TO FAMILY ROOM

OPEN TO KITCHEN

OPEN TO BELOW

BEDROOM 4
11'-0" X 11'-0"
8' C.H.

BEDROOM 3
12'-6" X 11'-0"
8' C.H. ③

MEMORIES . . .

'Seems everyone had a favorite uncle who drove a cool car... who had an endless supply of corny jokes... who picked you up and twirled you so fast the room seemed to spin. Wouldn't the wide open spaces in this family room be perfect for twirling?

NOTE: 9 ft. main level walls

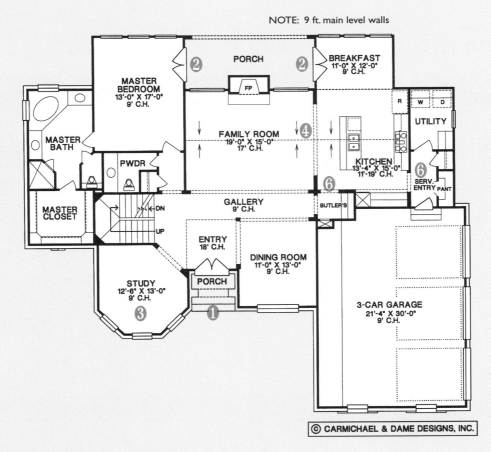

MASTER BEDROOM
13'-0" X 17'-0"
9' C.H.

PORCH

BREAKFAST
11'-0" X 12'-0"
9' C.H.

MASTER BATH

PWDR

MASTER CLOSET

FP

FAMILY ROOM
19'-0" X 15'-0"
17' C.H. ④

R W D

UTILITY

KITCHEN
13'-4" X 15'-0"
11'-19" C.H.

SERV. ENTRY ⑥

PANT.

DN

UP

GALLERY
9' C.H.

BUTLER'S ⑥

ENTRY
18' C.H.

DINING ROOM
11'-0" X 13'-0"
9' C.H.

STUDY
12'-6" X 13'-0"
9' C.H. ③

PORCH ①

3-CAR GARAGE
21'-4" X 30'-0"
9' C.H.

© CARMICHAEL & DAME DESIGNS, INC.

THE GREATWOOD SHOWCASE

1 With a full bath nearby, the study in the front of the home could easily be converted to another bedroom.

2 A spacious kitchen with walk-in pantry and angled snack bar is adjoined by a sunny breakfast area with access to the back porch.

3 An upstairs playroom offers built in shelves and a walk-in closet for toys.

4 With a 12-foot-high ceiling and a back wall of windows, this open family room seems even larger than it is.

5 This master suite enjoys special ceiling detail, access to the back porch, his and her vanities and a large walk-in closet.

6 Ample storage is available on the second floor over the garage.

PLAN HPT040052

Type: 1½-Story
First Floor: 1,924 square feet
Second Floor: 741 square feet
Total: 2,665 square feet
Bedrooms: 4
Bathrooms: 3
Width: 50'-7" **Depth:** 70'-4½"

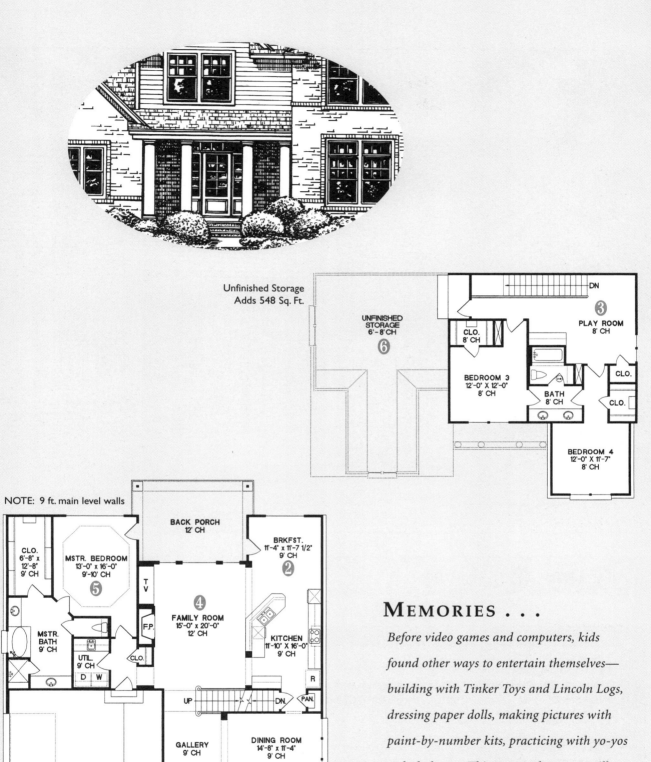

Unfinished Storage
Adds 548 Sq. Ft.

UNFINISHED
STORAGE
6'-8' CH
6

DN

PLAY ROOM
8' CH
3

CLO.
8' CH

CLO.

CLO.

BEDROOM 3
12'-0" X 12'-0"
8' CH

BATH
8' CH

BEDROOM 4
12'-0" X 11'-7"
8' CH

NOTE: 9 ft. main level walls

BACK PORCH
12' CH

BRKFST.
11'-4" x 11'-7 1/2"
9' CH
2

CLO.
6'-8" x
12'-8"
9' CH

MSTR. BEDROOM
13'-0" x 16'-0"
9'-10" CH
5

TV

FAMILY ROOM
15'-0" x 20'-0"
12' CH
4

KITCHEN
11'-10" X 16'-0"
9' CH

F.P.

MSTR.
BATH
9' CH

UTIL.
9' CH

D W

CLO.

R

UP

DN

PAN.

3-CAR
GARAGE
23'-10" X 32'-0"
9' CH

GALLERY
9' CH

DINING ROOM
14'-8" x 11'-4"
9' CH

ENTRY
9' CH

CLO.

BATH
9' CH

CLO.

1

STUDY/BEDROOM 2
12'-0" x 11'-0"
9' CH

MEMORIES . . .

Before video games and computers, kids found other ways to entertain themselves— building with Tinker Toys and Lincoln Logs, dressing paper dolls, making pictures with paint-by-number kits, practicing with yo-yos or hula hoops. This roomy play room will encourage creativity.

THE OLIVER

① The strong traditional lines and front porch on this home's facade will make it a welcome addition to any neighborhood.

② Just inside the entry, the flexible dining room/study makes this home adaptable to a variety of lifestyles.

③ An island counter is centrally located in the kitchen to shorten steps from the stove and sink.

④ A bright breakfast nook is flooded with natural light through bayed windows.

⑤ An 11-foot-high ceiling towers over the master bedroom with adjoining full bath and walk-in closet.

⑥ This large play room can be easily accessed by three upper-level bedrooms.

PLAN HPT040053

Type: 1½-Story
First Floor: 1,650 square feet
Second Floor: 1,038 square feet
Total: 2,688 square feet
Bedrooms: 4
Bathrooms: 3½
Width: 50'-0" **Depth:** 60'-0"

Memories . . .

Remember your best friend from childhood? You shared knock-knock jokes and deep secrets. You squabbled over who got to be the cop and who'd be the crook... or whose turn it was to be the mom. Imagine the fun you could have had in this roomy playroom.

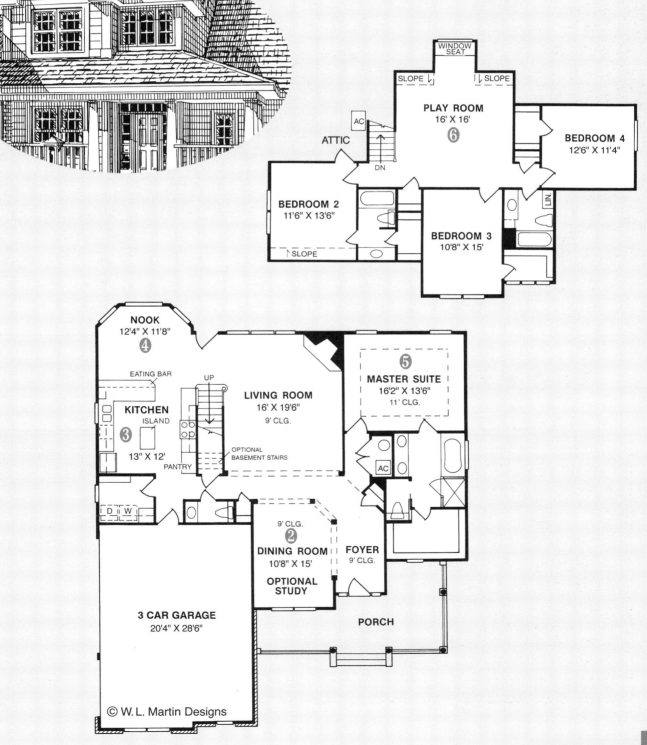

WINDOW SEAT

SLOPE   SLOPE

PLAY ROOM
16' X 16'
⑥

AC

ATTIC

DN

BEDROOM 4
12'6" X 11'4"

BEDROOM 2
11'6" X 13'6"

LIN.

BEDROOM 3
10'8" X 15'

SLOPE

SLOPE

NOOK
12'4" X 11'8"
④

EATING BAR

UP

LIVING ROOM
16' X 19'6"
9' CLG.

⑤

MASTER SUITE
16'2" X 13'6"
11' CLG.

KITCHEN
ISLAND
③
13" X 12"

OPTIONAL
BASEMENT STAIRS

PANTRY

AC

D W

DINING ROOM
10'8" X 15'
9' CLG.
②

FOYER
9' CLG.

OPTIONAL STUDY

3 CAR GARAGE
20'4" X 28'6"

PORCH

© W. L. Martin Designs

THE BRIDGEPORT

❶ The view from the volume entry includes a gracious staircase and formal living and dining rooms.

❷ Two built-in bookcases and a large window add interest to the living room.

❸ Three transom-topped windows and a raised hearth fireplace flanked by bookcases enhance the great room.

❹ A captivating gazebo dinette adjoins an island kitchen with huge pantry and two lazy Susans.

❺ Upstairs, three secondary bedrooms enjoy ample bathroom accommodations and a gallery in the corridor.

❻ On the main floor, the master bedroom boasts an arched window, cathedral ceiling and porch access.

PLAN HPT040054

Type: 1½-Story
First Floor: 1,881 square feet
Second Floor: 814 square feet
Total: 2,695 square feet
Bedrooms: 4
Bathrooms: 3½
Width: 72'-0" **Depth:** 45'-4"

MEMORIES . . .

Summer used to mean little league baseball, swimming lessons, camp, and reading dozens of books. The library sponsored a summer reading contest to teach us to love to read. With five sets of bookshelves, this house is perfect for grown-up book lovers.

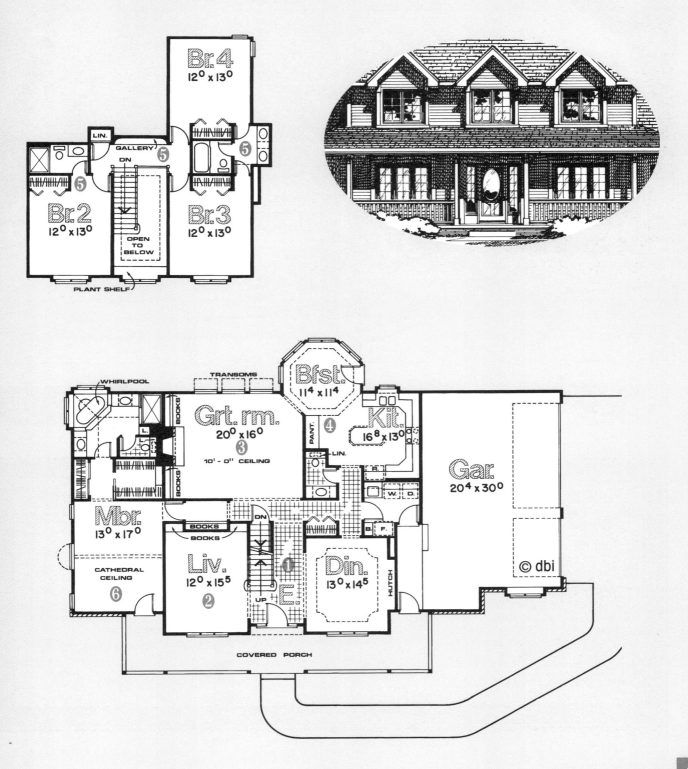

Br.4
$12^0 \times 13^0$

LIN.

GALLERY   5

DN

5

5

5

Br.2
$12^0 \times 13^0$

Br.3
$12^0 \times 13^0$

OPEN
TO
BELOW

PLANT SHELF

WHIRLPOOL

TRANSOMS

Bfst.
$11^4 \times 11^4$

Grt. rm.
$20^0 \times 16^0$
3

10' - 0" CEILING

BOOKS

BOOKS

PANT.

4

Kit.
$16^8 \times 13^0$

LIN.

W. D.

Gar.
$20^4 \times 30^0$

© dbi

Mbr.
$13^0 \times 17^0$

BOOKS

BOOKS

DN

B. F.

CATHEDRAL
CEILING

6

Liv.
$12^0 \times 15^5$

2

1

UP

Din.
$13^0 \times 14^5$

HUTCH

COVERED   PORCH

DESIGNERS'INK

THE RESTON

❶ This uncomplicated elevation complements the effortless floor plan inside.

❷ The master suite is a haven worth retreating to with its private sitting area offering a cozy window sill and built-in bookshelves.

❸ A corner whirlpool tub and compartmented shower offer escape in the master bath.

❹ A fireplace in the family room welcomes those in the kitchen and breakfast area.

❺ Bedroom 4 makes a wonderful guest suite offering its own bath.

❻ A large bonus room is beneficial for storage or if living space is desired.

PLAN HPT040055

Type: 1½-Story
First Floor: 1,901 square feet
Second Floor: 837 square feet
Total: 2,738 square feet
Bedrooms: 4
Bathrooms: 3½
Width: 69'-4" **Depth:** 53'-4"

MEMORIES . . .

When you were young you checked out a bag full of library books, then hurried home and let them take you to faraway worlds. No doubt you no longer have time to read a bag of books. But the secluded sitting area in this master bedroom will help you make the most of the time you have to get away from it all.

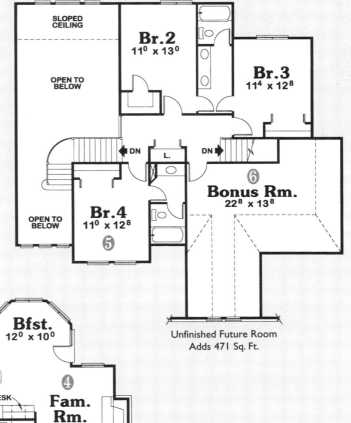

SLOPED CEILING

OPEN TO BELOW

Br. 2
11^0 x 13^0

Br. 3
11^4 x 12^8

DN

DN

L.

OPEN TO BELOW

Br. 4
11^0 x 12^8

⑤

⑥
Bonus Rm.
22^8 x 13^8

Unfinished Future Room
Adds 471 Sq. Ft.

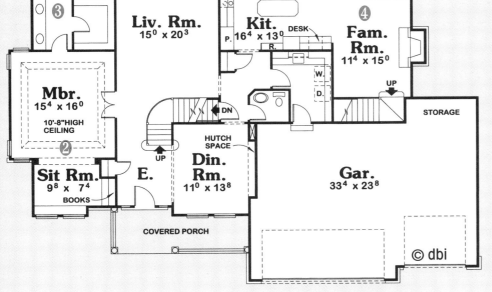

WHIRL-POOL

③

14'-5"HIGH CEILING

Liv. Rm.
15^0 x 20^3

Bfst.
12^0 x 10^0

Kit.
P. 16^4 x 13^0

DESK

④

Fam. Rm.
11^4 x 15^0

R.

W.

D.

UP

Mbr.
15^4 x 16^0

10'-8"HIGH CEILING

②

DN

UP

HUTCH SPACE

STORAGE

Sit Rm.
9^8 x 7^4

BOOKS

E.

Din. Rm.
11^0 x 13^8

Gar.
33^4 x 23^8

© dbi

COVERED PORCH

NOTE: 9 ft. main level walls

THE TIMBER CREST

① French doors and two columns add elegance in the dining room.

② An arched opening introduces the kitchen with walk-in pantry, ample cabinets and angled snack bar.

③ In the family room, an abundance of windows, a cathedral ceiling and a corner fireplace provide interest.

④ The second floor balcony offers views to the family room and the entry area.

⑤ Unfinished storage is available off the second floor hall.

⑥ Second floor bedrooms are served by two full baths.

PLAN HPT040056

Type: 1½-Story
First Floor: 1,907 square feet
Second Floor: 908 square feet
Total: 2,815 square feet
Bedrooms: 4
Bathrooms: 3½
Width: 64'-8" **Depth:** 51'-0"

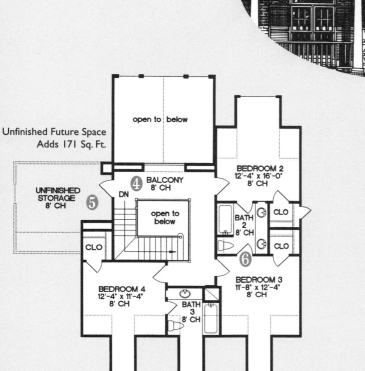

Unfinished Future Space
Adds 171 Sq. Ft.

UNFINISHED
STORAGE
8' CH ⑤

open to below

④ BALCONY
8' CH

DN

open to below

CLO

BEDROOM 2
12'-4" x 16'-0"
8' CH

BATH
2
8' CH

CLO

CLO

⑥

BEDROOM 4
12'-4" x 11'-4"
8' CH

BATH
3
8' CH

BEDROOM 3
11'-8" x 12'-4"
8' CH

MEMORIES . . .

If you were like most kids, you couldn't wait to get home from school. Home was a refuge where you were understood, accepted and loved—where you wore comfortable clothes and focused on your own brand of fun. This home has an air of warmth and welcome even grownups will love to come home to.

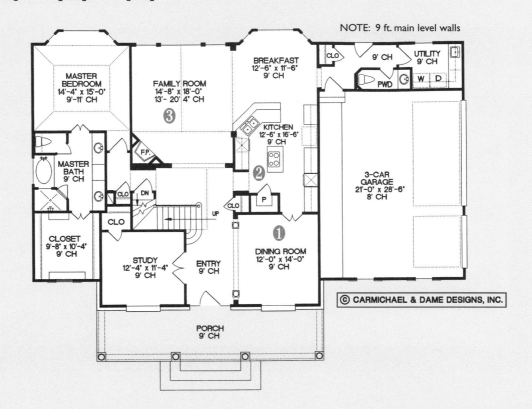

NOTE: 9 ft. main level walls

MASTER
BEDROOM
14'-4" x 15'-0"
9'-11" CH

FAMILY ROOM
14'-8" x 18'-0"
13'- 20' 4" CH
③

BREAKFAST
12'-6" x 11'-6"
9' CH

CLO

9' CH

UTILITY
9' CH

W. D.

PWD

MASTER
BATH
9' CH

F.P.

KITCHEN
12'-6" x 16'-6"
9' CH

②

3-CAR
GARAGE
21'-0" x 28'-6"
8' CH

CLO

DN

CLO

CLO

UP

P

CLO

①

CLOSET
9'-8" x 10'-4"
9' CH

STUDY
12'-4" x 11'-4"
9' CH

ENTRY
9' CH

DINING ROOM
12'-0" x 14'-0"
9' CH

© CARMICHAEL & DAME DESIGNS, INC.

PORCH
9' CH

THE MAHONING

1 A sunny haven to relax in, the sun room off the breakfast area features three sides of glass.

2 A huge walk-in pantry and island cooktop in the kitchen free counter space for preparing meals.

3 Unfinished storage space creates the opportunity for a second floor bonus room.

4 All three second floor bedrooms have walk-in closets and private access to full baths.

5 Double doors seclude a privately located den with sloped ceiling.

6 A built-in work bench in the garage is handy for outdoor projects.

PLAN HPT040057

Type: 1½-Story
First Floor: 1,979 square feet
Second Floor: 847 square feet
Total: 2,826 square feet
Bedrooms: 4
Bathrooms: 3½
Width: 61'-0" **Depth:** 64'-4"

MEMORIES . . .

Remember Grandma's knack for growing things? The big, juicy strawberries she grew in her garden? The bouquets of fresh flowers she kept on her dining room table? The house plants that flourished on her kitchen windowsill? She would have loved the sun room in this house!

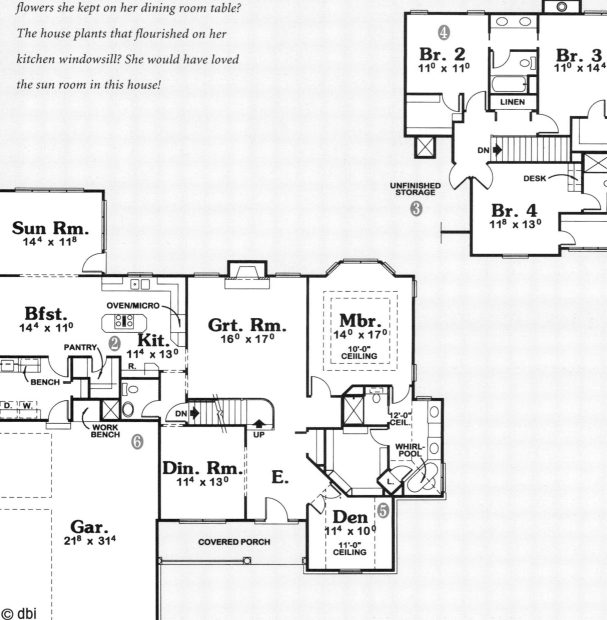

④

Br. 2
11^0 x 11^0

Br. 3
11^0 x 14^4

LINEN

DN

DESK

UNFINISHED STORAGE
③

Br. 4
11^8 x 13^0

Sun Rm.
14^4 x 11^8

Bfst.
14^4 x 11^0

OVEN/MICRO

②

PANTRY

Kit.
11^4 x 13^0

R.

BENCH

Grt. Rm.
16^0 x 17^0

Mbr.
14^0 x 17^0
10'-0" CEILING

D. W.

WORK BENCH

⑥

DN

UP

Din. Rm.
11^4 x 13^0

E.

12'-0" CEIL.

WHIRL-POOL

L.

Gar.
21^8 x 31^4

COVERED PORCH

Den
11^4 x 10^0
11'-0" CEILING

⑤

© dbi

NOTE: 9 ft. main level walls

THE ASHTON MANOR

① The visual appeal of this home is best expressed in an 8-sided family room with large rear and side windows, a see-thru fireplace, arched entry and 2-story ceiling.

② A dramatic curved staircase is viewed from a hall with 20-foot-high ceiling.

③ Unfinished storage is available off bedroom 2.

④ The master bedroom enjoys a special bayed sitting area, boxed ceiling and a luxurious bath.

⑤ All second floor bedrooms enjoy lovely sloped ceilings drawing focus to centrally located windows.

⑥ French doors in the study and breakfast area lead to a unique wraparound porch in the back of the home.

PLAN HPT040058

Type: 1½-Story
First Floor: 1,894 square feet
Second Floor: 936 square feet
Total: 2,830 square feet
Bedrooms: 4
Bathrooms: 3½
Width: 54'-7" **Depth:** 69'-7½"

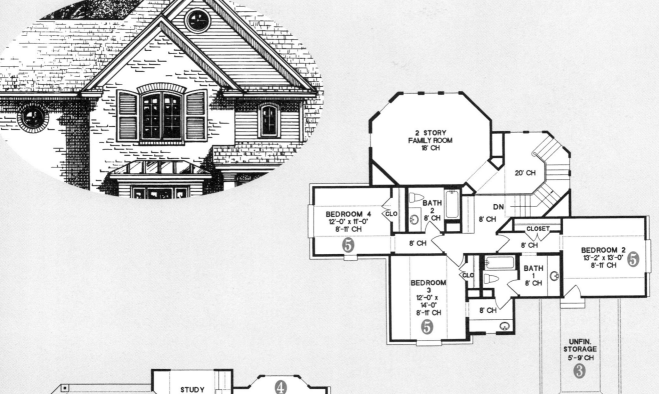

2 STORY
FAMILY ROOM
18' CH

20' CH

DN
8' CH

BEDROOM 4
12'-0" x 11'-0"
8'-11" CH

CLO

BATH
2
8' CH

8' CH

8' CH

CLOSET

8' CH

BEDROOM 2
13'-2" x 13'-0"
8'-11" CH

CLO

BATH
1
8' CH

BEDROOM
3
12'-0" x
14'-0"
8'-11" CH

8' CH

UNFIN.
STORAGE
5'-9' CH

Unfinished Storage
Adds 232 Sq. Ft.

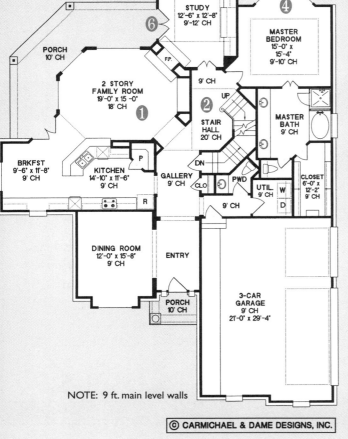

STUDY
12'-6" x 12'-8"
9'-12' CH

MASTER
BEDROOM
15'-0" x
15'-4"
9'-10' CH

PORCH
10' CH

9' CH

FP.

2 STORY
FAMILY ROOM
19'-0" x 15'-0"
18' CH

STAIR
HALL
20' CH

UP

MASTER
BATH
9' CH

BRKFST
9'-6" x 11'-8"
9' CH

KITCHEN
14'-10" x 11'-6"
9' CH

P

DN

GALLERY
9' CH

CLO

PWD

UTIL.
9' CH

W
D

CLOSET
6'-0" x
12'-2"
9' CH

R

9' CH

DINING ROOM
12'-0" x 15'-8"
9' CH

ENTRY

PORCH
10' CH

3-CAR
GARAGE
9' CH
21'-0" x 29'-4"

NOTE: 9 ft. main level walls

© CARMICHAEL & DAME DESIGNS, INC.

MEMORIES . . .

*Great aunts. They always seemed to get up
at the crack of dawn—thought that was the
best time of the day, when every thing was
fresh and quiet. With a door off the breakfast
area, this wraparound porch would make a
perfect place to watch the sunrise and greet
a new day.*

THE PEMBROOK

❶ A stucco and brick combination on the exterior adds to this home's stately appeal.

❷ Two walls of windows brighten a retreat in the master suite, providing a place for reading or quiet relaxation.

❸ A back porch is a wonderful place to enjoy the outdoors when entertaining.

❹ Storage space is provided in the garage for lawn and garden equipment.

❺ Whether studying or playing games, children will enjoy the open study and play room on the second level.

❻ A second floor walkway is visible inside this home's 2-story entry and family room.

PLAN HPT040059

Type: 1½-Story
First Floor: 2,101 square feet
Second Floor: 877 square feet
Total: 2,978 square feet
Bedrooms: 4
Bathrooms: 3
Width: 66'-0" **Depth:** 51'-0"

MEMORIES . . .

Remember when the first instrument kids learned to play was the accordion? And most families had someone taking tap dance or baton twirling lessons? Today, children are more likely to study guitar, ballet and karate. The combined study and play room area in this home would make a great place to practice.

BEDROOM 3
11'4" X 12'6"

OPEN TO BELOW

RAIL

WALKWAY

STUDY
12'6" X 10'10"

DN ⑤

RAIL

⑥

OPEN TO BELOW

PLAY ROOM
13'8" X 11'6"

BEDROOM 4
11'4" X 12'8"

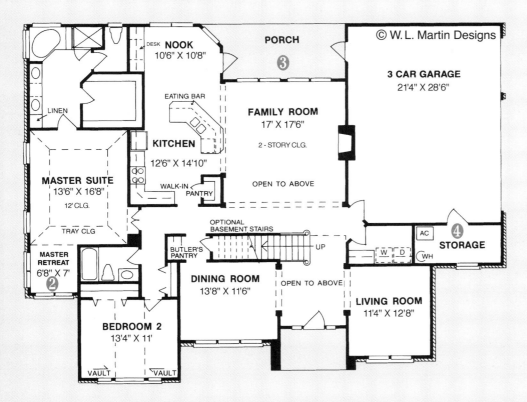

DESK **NOOK**
10'6" X 10'8"

PORCH
③

© W. L. Martin Designs

3 CAR GARAGE
21'4" X 28'6"

EATING BAR

KITCHEN
12'6" X 14'10"

FAMILY ROOM
17' X 17'6"

2 - STORY CLG.

LINEN

WALK-IN
PANTRY

OPEN TO ABOVE

MASTER SUITE
13'6" X 16'8"

12' CLG.

TRAY CLG

OPTIONAL
BASEMENT STAIRS

UP

AC

④ **STORAGE**

W D WH

**MASTER
RETREAT**
6'8" X 7'

②

BUTLER'S
PANTRY

DINING ROOM
13'8" X 11'6"

OPEN TO ABOVE

LIVING ROOM
11'4" X 12'8"

BEDROOM 2
13'4" X 11'

VAULT   VAULT

THE MIDDLEBORO

1 Toned-down window treatments and sturdy columns bring warmth to the front elevation.

2 French doors leading to the master bath reveal a large walk-in closet with ample storage space.

3 The three-car, side-load garage has the perfect place for a built-in workbench.

4 Whether an exercise room or study, the storage room caters to the individual needs of any family.

5 Each second floor bedroom has convenient access to a full bath and offers a walk-in closet.

6 Ten-foot main level walls provide an old-home openness to main level rooms.

PLAN HPT040060

Type: 1½-Story
First Floor: 2,072 square feet
Second Floor: 917 square feet
Total: 2,989 square feet
Bedrooms: 4
Bathrooms: 3½
Width: 68'-0" **Depth:** 55'-8"

MEMORIES . . .

Remember the old days when everyone in the family shared one bathroom? The pounding on the door when it was finally your turn? Back then, a home with three-and-a-half baths would have seemed too good to be true!

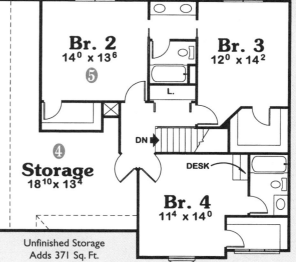

Br. 2 14⁰ x 13⁶ ⑤

Br. 3 12⁰ x 14²

L.

DN

DESK

Storage 18¹⁰ x 13⁴ ④

Br. 4 11⁴ x 14⁰

Unfinished Storage
Adds 371 Sq. Ft.

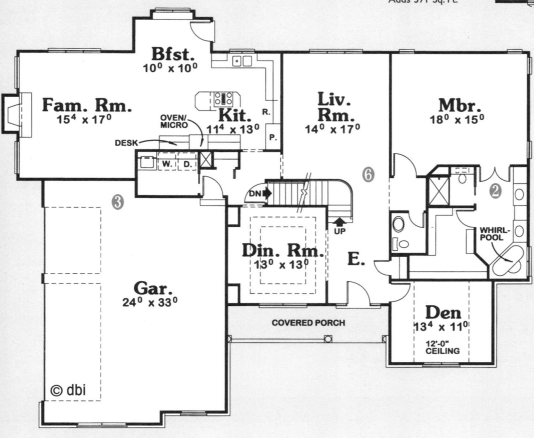

Bfst. 10⁰ x 10⁰

Fam. Rm. 15⁴ x 17⁰

OVEN/MICRO

Kit. 11⁴ x 13⁰

R.

P.

DESK

W. D.

Liv. Rm. 14⁰ x 17⁰

Mbr. 18⁰ x 15⁰

⑥

②

WHIRL-POOL

③

DN

UP

Din. Rm. 13⁰ x 13⁰

E.

Gar. 24⁰ x 33⁰

© dbi

COVERED PORCH

Den 13⁴ x 11⁰

12'-0" CEILING

NOTE: 10 ft. main level walls

THE MARLOW

① A plant shelf and arched transom window decorate the entry of this appealing home.

② A fireplace and cathedral ceiling are highlights in the den, located just inside the entry.

③ A tall window grouping offers a dramatic view from the great room, with double doors leading outside.

④ French doors seclude the dining room from the informal area of the home.

⑤ Just off the sunny breakfast area, the warm hearth room is a natural place to relax.

⑥ The gourmet kitchen includes a unique double island, walk-in pantry and plenty of counter space.

PLAN HPT040061

Type: 1½-Story
First Floor: 2,215 square feet
Second Floor: 825 square feet
Total: 3,040 square feet
Bedrooms: 4
Bathrooms: 3½
Width: 66'-0" **Depth:** 66'-0"

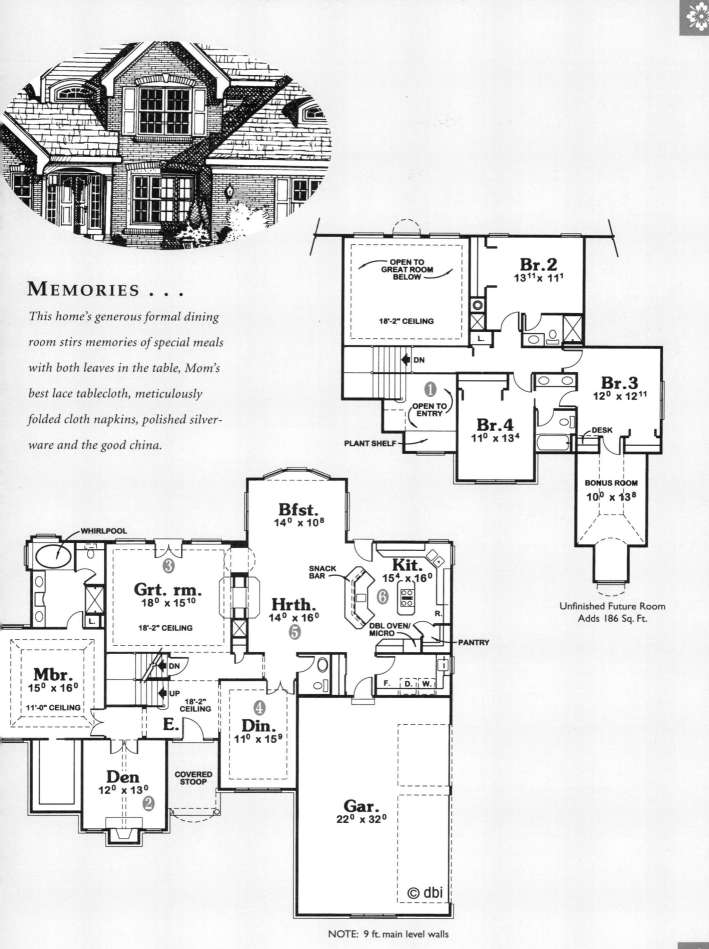

MEMORIES . . .

This home's generous formal dining room stirs memories of special meals with both leaves in the table, Mom's best lace tablecloth, meticulously folded cloth napkins, polished silverware and the good china.

OPEN TO GREAT ROOM BELOW

18'-2" CEILING

Br.2
13¹¹ x 11¹

DN

①

OPEN TO ENTRY

PLANT SHELF

Br.4
11⁰ x 13⁴

L.

Br.3
12⁰ x 12¹¹

DESK

BONUS ROOM
10⁰ x 13⁸

Unfinished Future Room
Adds 186 Sq. Ft.

WHIRLPOOL

③

Grt. rm.
18⁰ x 15¹⁰

18'-2" CEILING

Bfst.
14⁰ x 10⁸

SNACK BAR

Kit.
15⁴ x 16⁰

⑥

R.

DBL OVEN/ MICRO

PANTRY

Hrth.
14⁰ x 16⁰

⑤

L.

Mbr.
15⁰ x 16⁰

11'-0" CEILING

DN

UP

18'-2" CEILING

E.

④

Din.
11⁰ x 15⁹

F. D. W.

Den
12⁰ x 13⁰

②

COVERED STOOP

Gar.
22⁰ x 32⁰

© dbi

NOTE: 9 ft. main level walls

THE TEALWOOD ESTATES

❶ A wrap-around porch and three dormers add interest to this elevation.

❷ French doors in the dining room and study provide style and access to the porch.

❸ In the family room, cathedral ceilings center on the fireplace which is also flanked by windows.

❹ The upstairs balcony provides dramatic views to the family room and entry.

❺ All secondary bedrooms enjoy window seats tucked in dormers.

❻ Three walk-in closets provide plenty of storage on the second level.

PLAN HPT040062

Type: 1½-Story
First Floor: 2,116 square feet
Second Floor: 956 square feet
Total: 3,072 square feet
Bedrooms: 4
Bathrooms: 3½
Width: 67'-8" **Depth:** 53'-0"

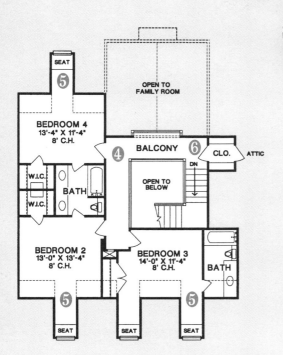

SEAT
5

BEDROOM 4
13'-4" X 11'-4"
8' C.H.

OPEN TO
FAMILY ROOM

4 BALCONY **6** CLO. ATTIC

W.I.C.

OPEN TO
BELOW

DN

BATH

W.I.C.

BEDROOM 2
13'-0" X 13'-4"
8' C.H.

BEDROOM 3
14'-0" X 11'-4"
8' C.H.

BATH

5

SEAT

5

SEAT

5

SEAT

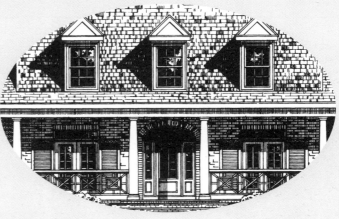

MEMORIES . . .

The lovely balcony in this home stirs visions of pajama-clad children with heads pressed against another set of spindles—straining to listen to Mother and Father discuss a recent request or watching the chatter and laughter when they had company.

NOTE: 9 ft. main level walls

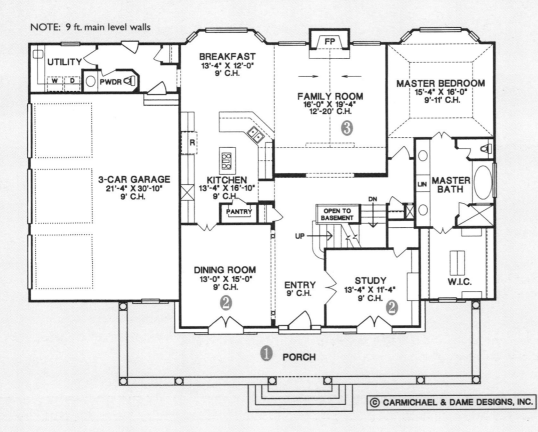

UTILITY

W D **PWDR**

FP

BREAKFAST
13'-4" X 12'-0"
9' C.H.

FAMILY ROOM
16'-0" X 19'-4"
12'-20' C.H.

3

MASTER BEDROOM
15'-4" X 16'-0"
9'-11' C.H.

R

3-CAR GARAGE
21'-4" X 30'-10"
9' C.H.

KITCHEN
13'-4" X 16'-10"
9' C.H.

PANTRY

LIN

MASTER BATH

OPEN TO
BASEMENT

DN

UP

DINING ROOM
13'-0" X 15'-0"
9' C.H.

2

ENTRY
9' C.H.

STUDY
13'-4" X 11'-4"
9' C.H.

2

W.I.C.

1 **PORCH**

© CARMICHAEL & DAME DESIGNS, INC.

THE PARKGATE SHOWCASE

① French doors open to a raised study located midway up the home's U-shaped staircase.

② A dramatic 2-story entry views a formal dining room and open staircase.

③ A butler's pantry conveniently located between the kitchen and dining room simplifies entertaining.

④ The centrally located family room features an elaborate angled ceiling, towering windows, fireplace and built-in cabinetry.

⑤ Extra storage space in the garage provides an ideal spot for lawn and sports equipment.

⑥ A huge storage area is available over the garage on the second floor.

PLAN HPT040063

Type: 1½-Story
First Floor: 2,060 square feet
Second Floor: 1,020 square feet
Total: 3,080 square feet
Bedrooms: 4
Bathrooms: 3½
Width: 68'-3" **Depth:** 55'-9"

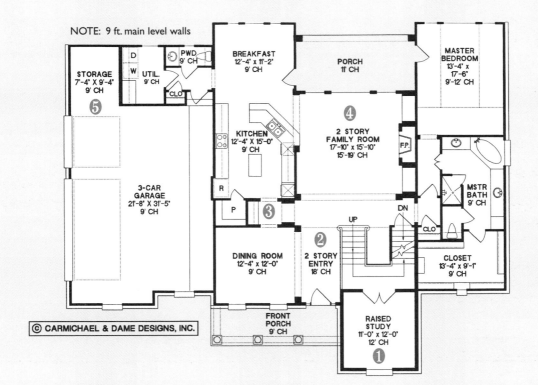

BEDROOM 3
12'-4" x 14'-0"
8'-10" CH

2 STORY FAMILY ROOM
15'-19' CH

CLO

BEDROOM 2
13'-5 1/2" x 12'-10"
8' CH

CLO

BATH 3
8' CH

BATH 2
8' CH

8' CH

DN

UNFINISHED STORAGE
⑥

BEDROOM 4
10'-8" x 14'-8"
8'-10" CH

CLO

OPEN TO BELOW

RAISED STUDY
11'-0" x 12'-0"
12' CH

Unfinished Storage
Adds 493 Sq. Ft.

MEMORIES . . .

When we were children, summer nights meant chasing fireflies, playing hide 'n seek in the dark, identifying the constellations and licking double-deck ice cream cones before they melted. With a porch facing the backyard, the whole family will enjoy summer nights again.

NOTE: 9 ft. main level walls

STORAGE
7'-4" X 9'-4"
9' CH
⑤

D
W

UTIL.
9' CH

CLO

PWD.
9' CH

BREAKFAST
12'-4" x 11'-2"
9' CH

PORCH
11' CH

MASTER BEDROOM
13'-4" x 17'-6"
9'-12' CH

KITCHEN
12'-4" X 15'-0"
9' CH

2 STORY FAMILY ROOM
17'-10" x 15'-10"
15'-19' CH

④

F.P.

3-CAR GARAGE
21'-8" X 31'-5"
9' CH

R

P

③

MSTR BATH
9' CH

CLO

DINING ROOM
12'-4" x 12'-0"
9' CH

2 STORY ENTRY
18' CH

②

UP

DN

CLOSET
13'-4" x 9'-1"
9' CH

ⓒ CARMICHAEL & DAME DESIGNS, INC.

FRONT PORCH
9' CH

RAISED STUDY
11'-0" x 12'-0"
12' CH
①

THE KEMPTON COURT

1 An upper level porch and bayed turret contribute to this home's castle-like demeanor.

2 A bayed study can function as entertaining space when coupled with the dining and living rooms.

3 An octagon shaped living room is enhanced by a vaulted ceiling, large fireplace and special window details.

4 The master bedroom enjoys an elaborate vaulted ceiling and access to the back porch.

5 A spacious master bath features his and her closets, twin vanities and arched ceiling over a whirlpool tub.

6 Upstairs, a lengthy balcony provides a spectacular view to the living room and open staircase.

PLAN HPT040064

Type: 1½-Story
First Floor: 2,112 square feet
Second Floor: 982 square feet
Total: 3,094 square feet
Bedrooms: 4
Bathrooms: 3½
Width: 67'-1" **Depth:** 65'-10⅛"

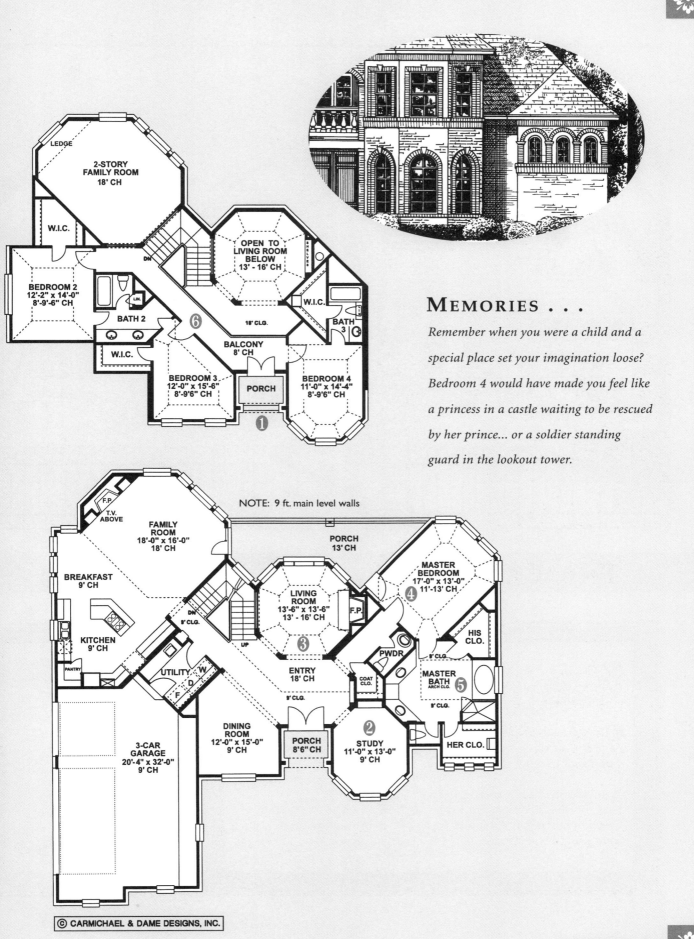

LEDGE

2-STORY
FAMILY ROOM
18' CH

W.I.C.

BEDROOM 2
12'-2" x 14'-0"
8'-9'-6" CH

BATH 2

W.I.C.

OPEN TO
LIVING ROOM
BELOW
13' - 16' CH

W.I.C.

BATH 3

DN

LIN.

❻

18' CLG.

BALCONY
8' CH

BEDROOM 3
12'-0" x 15'-6"
8'-9'6" CH

PORCH

BEDROOM 4
11'-0" x 14'-4"
8'-9'6" CH

❶

MEMORIES . . .

Remember when you were a child and a special place set your imagination loose? Bedroom 4 would have made you feel like a princess in a castle waiting to be rescued by her prince... or a soldier standing guard in the lookout tower.

F.P.

T.V.
ABOVE

FAMILY
ROOM
18'-0" x 16'-0"
18' CH

BREAKFAST
9' CH

KITCHEN
9' CH

PANTRY

UTILITY

W
D
F

DN

9' CLG.

UP

NOTE: 9 ft. main level walls

PORCH
13' CH

LIVING
ROOM
13'-6" x 13'-6"
13' - 16' CH

F.P.

❸

ENTRY
18' CH

9' CLG.

COAT
CLO.

PWDR

MASTER
BEDROOM
17'-0" x 13'-0"
11'-13' CH

❹

HIS
CLO.

9' CLG.

MASTER
BATH
ARCH CLG.

❺

9' CLG.

3-CAR
GARAGE
20'-4" x 32'-0"
9' CH

DINING
ROOM
12'-0" x 15'-0"
9' CH

PORCH
8'6" CH

STUDY
11'-0" x 13'-0"
9' CH

❷

HER CLO.

© CARMICHAEL & DAME DESIGNS, INC.

THE ELEANOR

1 A Georgian influence gives this design a sense of timelessness and prominence.

2 Coat closets and formal rooms flank the entry, making this area convenient for entertaining.

3 An informal family area at the rear of the home features a bayed breakfast area, snack bar and raised hearth fireplace.

4 His and her closets, built-in dressers and a luxurious whirlpool tub enhanced by bayed windows highlight a pampering master suite.

5 All second-floor bedrooms provide access to walk-in closets—great for the storage of toys.

6 Bedroom 4 easily converts into a study and showcases a gorgeous balcony that views the family room.

PLAN HPT040065

Type: 1¹/₂-Story
First Floor: 2,130 square feet
Second Floor: 973 square feet
Total: 3,103 square feet
Bedrooms: 4
Bathrooms: 4¹/₂
Width: 78'-0" **Depth:** 45'-4"

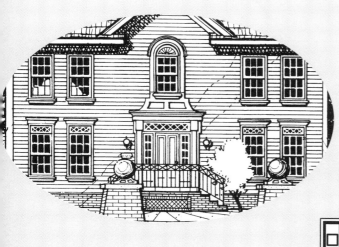

MEMORIES . . .

This sunny breakfast area calls to mind activities that took place on the kitchen table of your childhood home—cutting out home-made Valentines, coloring Easter eggs, making paper mache' school projects and decorating Christmas tree cookies.

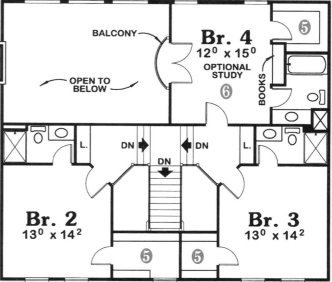

BALCONY

Br. 4
12^0 x 15^0

⑤

OPEN TO
BELOW

OPTIONAL
STUDY

⑥

BOOKS

L.   DN   DN   L.

DN

Br. 2
13^0 x 14^2

⑤   ⑤

Br. 3
13^0 x 14^2

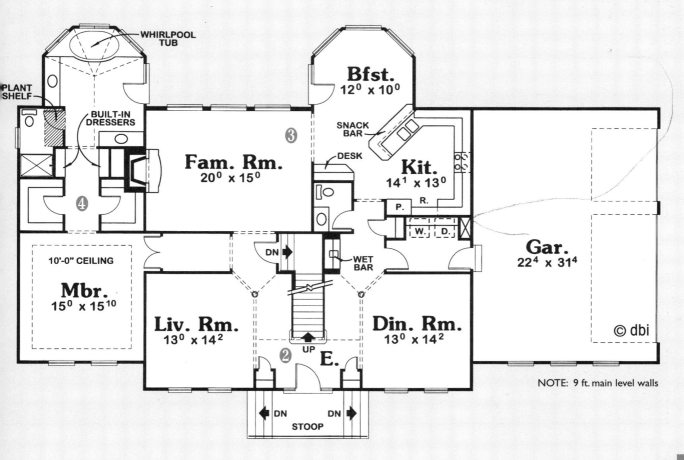

WHIRLPOOL
TUB

PLANT
SHELF

BUILT-IN
DRESSERS

Bfst.
12^0 x 10^0

SNACK
BAR

③

Fam. Rm.
20^0 x 15^0

DESK

Kit.
14^1 x 13^0

P.   R.

④

W.   D.

Gar.
22^4 x 31^4

© dbi

10'-0" CEILING

Mbr.
15^0 x 15^{10}

DN

WET
BAR

Liv. Rm.
13^0 x 14^2

②   UP   **E.**

Din. Rm.
13^0 x 14^2

DN   DN
STOOP

NOTE: 9 ft. main level walls

THE CLAYTON

❶ A glimpse of the great room's view can be enjoyed from the dining room and entry.

❷ The kitchen is open to the hearth room and breakfast area and features a snack bar and two pantries, one of which is a walk-in.

❸ Children in the hearth room or great room can easily access the second level via a rear staircase.

❹ Those working at home will benefit from built-in bookshelves in the den.

❺ Homeowners will enjoy time alone in the master suite with private sitting area, covered porch, built-in entertainment center, bookshelves and fireplace.

❻ With its own bath and walk-in closet, guests will enjoy the privacy of bedroom 2.

PLAN HPT040066

Type: 1½-Story
First Floor: 2,454 square feet
Second Floor: 986 square feet
Total: 3,440 square feet
Bedrooms: 4
Bathrooms: 3½
Width: 73'-4" **Depth:** 59'-4"

MEMORIES . . .

The stylish den off the entry reminds one of the room Mrs. Cleaver sent Beaver to for one of many heart-to-heart talks with Mr. Cleaver. It was the place Beaver had those famous breakthroughs in understanding. For some reason, Wally was rarely summoned there.

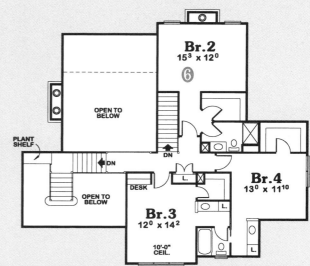

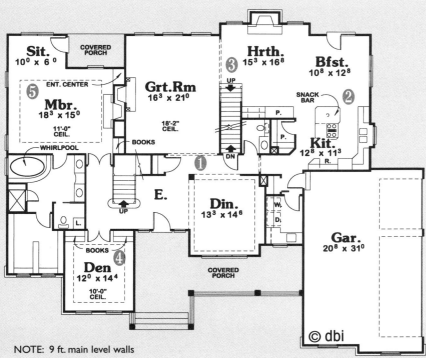

NOTE: 9 ft. main level walls

THE LANDRETH

1 A bayed window and gazebo on the front of this home create a friendly impression upon first view.

2 An elevated entry views the dining room past an open hand railing.

3 French doors are centered in the great room and lead outside.

4 The functional kitchen has a large island with cooktop and snack bar and views the breakfast area via three arched openings.

5 Twin entertainment centers encase the fireplace in the family room, which also has atrium-door access to the outdoors.

6 A loft on the second floor works well as a computer center and features double doors that open to view the two-story family room.

PLAN HPT040067

Type: 1½-Story
First Floor: 2,461 square feet
Second Floor: 1,019 square feet
Total: 3,480 square feet
Bedrooms: 4
Bathrooms: 3½
Width: 74'-0" **Depth:** 79'-6⅝"

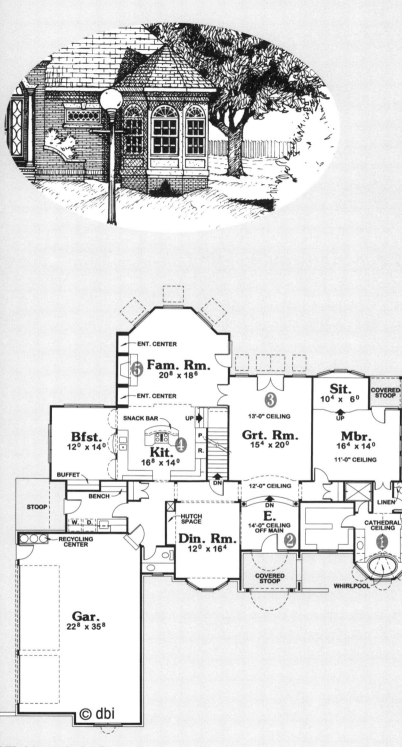

MEMORIES . . .

With a semi-circle transom and glamorous sidelights adorning the front door and an elevated, curved entry—with stately columns and graceful arched opening leading to the great room—it's not hard to visualize Scarlett standing in this doorway calling Rhett to come back.

ENT. CENTER

Fam. Rm.
$20^8 \times 18^6$

ENT. CENTER

SNACK BAR   UP

Bfst.
$12^0 \times 14^0$

Kit.
$16^8 \times 14^0$

P.

R.

13'-0" CEILING

Grt. Rm.
$15^4 \times 20^0$

Sit.
$10^4 \times 6^0$

UP

COVERED STOOP

Mbr.
$16^4 \times 14^0$

11'-0" CEILING

BUFFET

BENCH

STOOP

W.   D.

RECYCLING CENTER

HUTCH SPACE

Din. Rm.
$12^0 \times 16^4$

12'-0" CEILING

DN

E.
14'-0" CEILING OFF MAIN

DN

LINEN

CATHEDRAL CEILING

COVERED STOOP

WHIRLPOOL

Gar.
$22^8 \times 35^8$

© dbi

OTE: 9 ft. main level walls

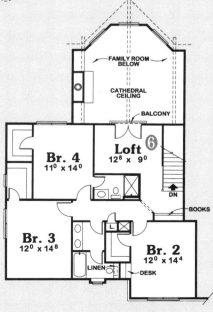

FAMILY ROOM BELOW

CATHEDRAL CEILING

BALCONY

Br. 4
$11^0 \times 14^0$

Loft
$12^8 \times 9^0$

DN

BOOKS

Br. 3
$12^0 \times 14^8$

L

DESK

Br. 2
$12^0 \times 14^4$

LINEN

In the
Nostalgia *Collection you will find...*

FLEXIBLE ROOMS

Because the same design may work equally well for an empty-nester and family, we've incorporated the use of a variety of flexible rooms in these home plans. While a room may be called out as a bedroom, we've designed it in such a way to suggest that it could be used as an office, exercise room or hobby room. These spaces can really serve a variety of functions and greatly benefit the homes' resale value.

ECONOMIC USE OF SPACE

Home buyers are continually looking for larger and larger storage areas. They're also looking for the most economical home for their dollar. So, in every inch of these homes, we tried to use the space that's available, especially the space directly under the roof. You'll find plenty of bonus rooms, attics, lofts and second-floor bedrooms with dormers to make the rooms more useable. And all but a few of these homes offer nine-foot main level walls. Buyers can use these spaces as they see fit and will also enjoy the aesthetic appeal since many of these areas create charming nooks with quaintly sloped ceilings.

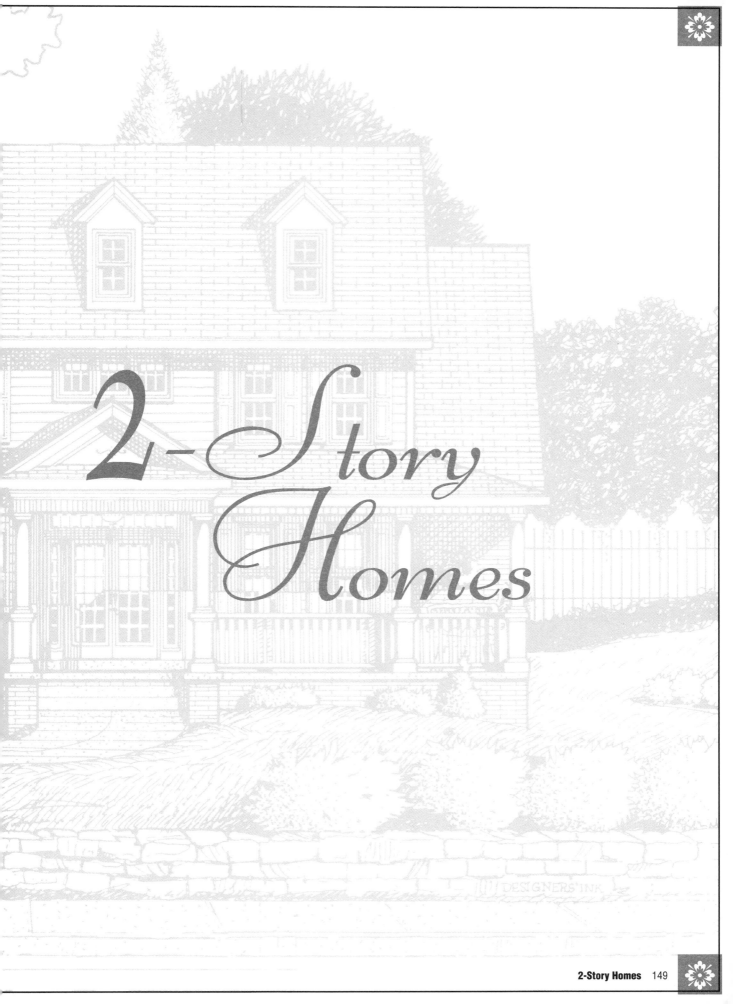

2-Story Homes

THE COPELAND

① This spacious family room features perfect windows for country tie-back curtains, an open staircase, beautiful fireplace and built-in entertainment center.

② A window above the sink, wrapping counters and a large walk-in pantry add convenience to this kitchen.

③ A bayed dining area provides access to the back yard and an adjoining coat closet.

④ Bedroom 2 is loaded with extras—an angled 10-foot ceiling, lovely arched window and walk-in closet.

⑤ Unfinished storage above the garage could also be converted into a hobby or exercise room.

PLAN HPT040068

Type: Two-Story
First Floor: 716 square feet
Second Floor: 747 square feet
Total: 1,463 square feet
Bedrooms: 3
Bathrooms: 2½
Width: 45'-4" **Depth:** 38'-0"

Memories . . .

This traditional looking home may stir memories of great times at grandma's house: the time she tipped over a couple of kitchen chairs which became imaginary hot rods, the picnic on her living room floor, the tent she helped you build under her dining room table.

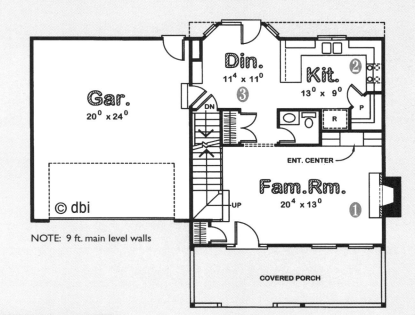

Gar.
20⁰ x 24⁰

© dbi

NOTE: 9 ft. main level walls

Din.
11⁴ x 11⁰ ③

Kit.
13⁰ x 9⁰ ②

P

R

ENT. CENTER

Fam.Rm.
20⁴ x 13⁰ ①

DN

UP

COVERED PORCH

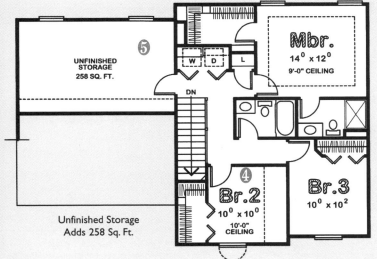

UNFINISHED STORAGE
258 SQ. FT. ⑤

W   D   L

DN

Mbr.
14⁰ x 12⁰
9'-0" CEILING

Unfinished Storage
Adds 258 Sq. Ft.

④ Br.2
10⁰ x 10⁰
10'-0" CEILING

Br.3
10⁰ x 10²

THE SILVERDALE

❶ A wraparound staircase adds style to the entry.

❷ The living room offers a full fireplace and a picture window that looks out onto the covered front porch.

❸ A great place for gathering family and friends, the spacious dining room has windows on two walls and a door to the back yard.

❹ Just off the kitchen, a covered porch provides a private place to relax outdoors.

❺ Ample storage is available on the second level, accessed off the hall.

❻ An extra storage area in the garage is a convenient place to store bikes and lawn equipment.

PLAN HPT040069

Type: Two-Story
First Floor: 749 square feet
Second Floor: 742 square feet
Total: 1,491 square feet
Bedrooms: 3
Bathrooms: 2½
Width: 39'-4" **Depth:** 47'-8"

MEMORIES . . .

The kitchen has always been the room we're most creative in. It's where we mixed lemonade to sell on the corner, formed Playdoh masterpieces, learned how to make the secret family recipe and carried out wacky experiments. This roomy kitchen is bound to inspire imagination for years to come.

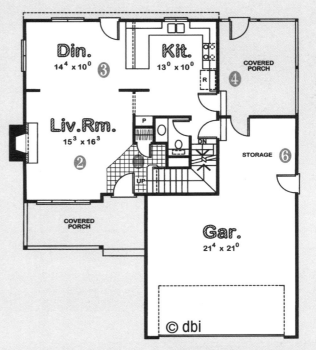

NOTE: 9 ft. main level walls

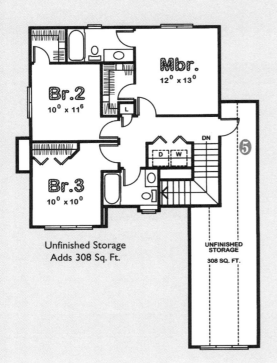

Unfinished Storage
Adds 308 Sq. Ft.

THE ALENHURST

1 Strategically located between the formal and informal eating areas, the kitchen features an island that shortens trips from the stove and sink.

2 Triple windows brighten the sunny breakfast area.

3 A large great room features a fireplace and has access to the second floor.

4 A cozy window seat on the second floor is a perfect spot for a rainy day.

5 A private bath and walk-in closet accompany the large master suite.

6 A rear staircase keeps traffic away from the formal dining room and entry.

PLAN HPT040070

Type: Two-Story
First Floor: 842 square feet
Second Floor: 722 square feet
Total: 1,564 square feet
Bedrooms: 3
Bathrooms: 2½
Width: 42'-0" **Depth:** 45'-4"

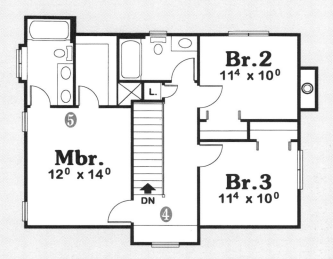

Br. 2
11⁴ x 10⁰

Mbr.
12⁰ x 14⁰

Br. 3
11⁴ x 10⁰

⑤

④

DN

MEMORIES . . .

The window seat on the second floor reminds one of times snuggling under a cozy quilt identifying shapes in the clouds, watching the rain come down, admiring a gorgeous sunset or counting the stars.

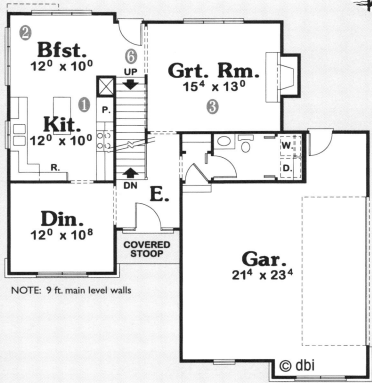

Bfst.
12⁰ x 10⁰

②

UP

Grt. Rm.
15⁴ x 13⁰

⑥

Kit.
12⁰ x 10⁰

①

P.

③

R.

W.

D.

DN

E.

Din.
12⁰ x 10⁸

**COVERED
STOOP**

Gar.
21⁴ x 23⁴

© dbi

NOTE: 9 ft. main level walls

THE SANDERS

① The covered porch of this home, together with a lovely transom window above the front door, create a desirable front elevation.

② Adding to the entry's impressive view of the French doors leading to a secluded den, is the beautiful staircase.

③ Three large windows and a raised hearth fireplace add character to the already inviting family room.

④ Wrapping counters in the kitchen are convenient for the chef of the house, as are a snack bar, lazy Susan and pantry.

⑤ The breakfast area resembles a cozy nook with access to the outside.

PLAN HPT040071

Type: Two-Story
First Floor: 874 square feet
Second Floor: 754 square feet
Total: 1,628 square feet
Bedrooms: 3
Bathrooms: 2½
Width: 49'-4" **Depth:** 33'-4"

Memories . . .

This kitchen's roomy snack bar brings back thoughts of happy times watching Mom prepare tasty delights, licking the beaters and being first on hand to sample the finished product.

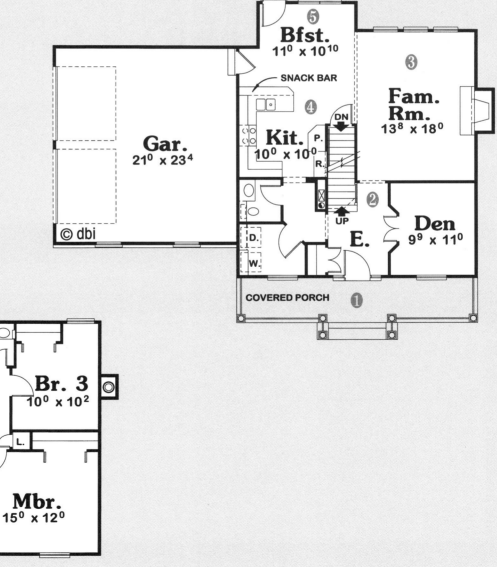

Gar.
$21^0 \times 23^4$

© dbi

Bfst.
$11^0 \times 10^{10}$

SNACK BAR

Fam. Rm.
$13^8 \times 18^0$

Kit.
$10^0 \times 10^0$

P.
R.

DN

UP

E.

Den
$9^9 \times 11^0$

D.
W.

COVERED PORCH

Br. 2
$10^0 \times 10^2$

DN

Br. 3
$10^0 \times 10^2$

L.

WHIRLPOOL

Mbr.
$15^0 \times 12^0$

THE LAVERTON

① A formal dining room with boxed window is open to entry.

② Also viewed from the entry, the great room has a lovely fireplace and large boxed window.

③ Open to the great room and kitchen, the breakfast area seems larger than it is. A patio door and built-in desk add convenience.

④ The well-laid out kitchen includes a boxed window above the sink and a pantry.

⑤ Complete with closet, the laundry just off the garage doubles as a mud room.

⑥ Beautiful arched window and sloped ceiling adorn bedroom 3.

PLAN HPT040072

Type: Two-Story
First Floor: 891 square feet
Second Floor: 759 square feet
Total: 1,650 square feet
Bedrooms: 3
Bathrooms: 2½
Width: 44'-0" **Depth:** 40'-0"

MEMORIES . . .

The prominent fireplace in this great room brings back images of falls past. Crisp, cool air with a smoky scent from fireplaces all over the neighborhood. Shuffling through leaves on the way home from school and jumping into the pile in our front yard. A warm light in the window that welcomed us home.

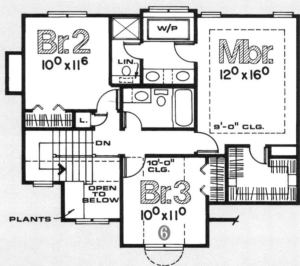

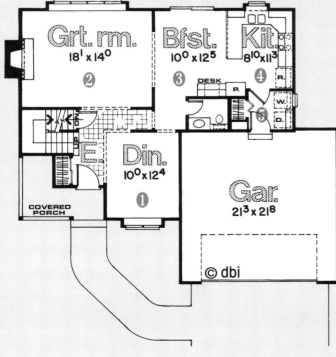

THE HOPEWELL

❶ A large covered porch welcomes you into this three bedroom, two-story home.

❷ A lovely fireplace anchors one end of the huge great room.

❸ On the other end, French doors open into a three-season porch, expanding the room even further for entertaining.

❹ Cozy corner dining turns the kitchen area into a great place for family meals or informal gatherings. A pantry adjoins the eating area, providing plenty of storage.

❺ Laundry facilities are conveniently located near the bedrooms on the second floor.

❻ There will be plenty of room for luggage, sports equipment and seasonal items in the huge unfinished storage area over the garage.

PLAN HPT040073

Type: Two-Story
First Floor: 846 square feet
Second Floor: 804 square feet
Total: 1,650 square feet
Bedrooms: 3
Bathrooms: 2½
Width: 52'-0" **Depth:** 37'-4"

MEMORIES . . .

If your home didn't have a piano, a relative's did. The kids played "Chopsticks" and original compositions (all loud); the teenagers played a little rock; the older folks played ballads and everyone sang carols around it at Christmas. This great room is large enough for a piano—and a lifetime of memories.

NOTE: 9 ft. main level walls

Gar.
21⁴ x 26⁰

© dbi

Kit.
12⁶ x 12⁴

Din.
11⁹ x 12⁴

DN   UP

Grt.Rm.
22¹¹ x 14⁸

3-SEASON PORCH

COVERED PORCH

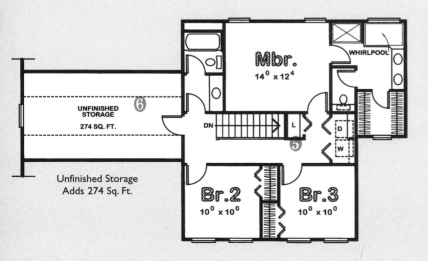

Mbr.
14⁰ x 12⁴

WHIRLPOOL

UNFINISHED STORAGE
274 SQ. FT.

DN   L

D
W

Br.2
10⁰ x 10⁰

Br.3
10⁰ x 10⁰

Unfinished Storage
Adds 274 Sq. Ft.

THE WEDGEPORT

1 Four upper-level windows and sidelights bring a feeling of openness to this home's 2-story entry.

2 Bayed windows offer beauty in the formal dining room, located next to the kitchen.

3 An angled eating bar was designed for an informal meal or to serve those in the living room.

4 A fireplace accents the rear view in the living room.

5 Amenities in the master suite include a walk-in closet, double vanity and whirlpool tub.

6 An organized utility area consists of a powder bath and laundry room with soaking sink and counter space for folding clothes.

PLAN HPT040074

Type: Two-Story
First Floor: 979 square feet
Second Floor: 710 square feet
Total: 1,689 square feet
Bedrooms: 3
Bathrooms: 2½
Width: 48'-0" **Depth:** 38'-0"

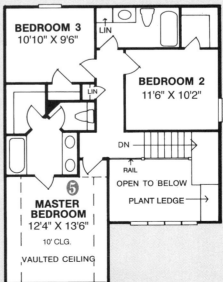

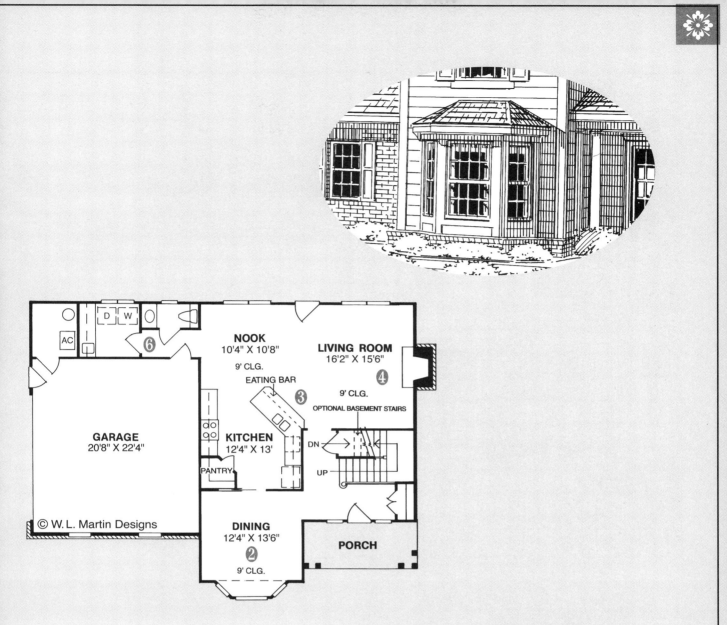

GARAGE
20'8" X 22'4"

© W. L. Martin Designs

NOOK
10'4" X 10'8"

9' CLG.

EATING BAR

KITCHEN
12'4" X 13'

PANTRY

DINING
12'4" X 13'6"

9' CLG.

LIVING ROOM
16'2" X 15'6"

9' CLG.

OPTIONAL BASEMENT STAIRS

DN

UP

PORCH

MEMORIES . . .

This home's timeless charm stirs memories of simpler times when gas was fifty cents a gallon, apples were a quarter a pound and candy bars were a dime. It was a time when ladies wore white gloves and pillbox hats and the calendar on the kitchen wall had little on it besides birthdays and anniversaries.

BEDROOM 3
10'10" X 9'6"

LIN

LIN

BEDROOM 2
11'6" X 10'2"

DN

RAIL

OPEN TO BELOW

PLANT LEDGE

MASTER
BEDROOM
12'4" X 13'6"

10' CLG.

VAULTED CEILING

THE ACKERLY

1 A large covered stoop opens to an informal floor plan with the kitchen located to the front.

2 A snack bar serves the dinette, which could function both formally and informally.

3 A media room—perfect for a family work area with home computer—could also become a dining room or hobby area.

4 A cathedral ceiling centers on the fireplace in the dramatic family room.

5 A nook in the master bedroom can be used an as entertainment center or bookshelf.

PLAN HPT040075

Type: Two-Story
First Floor: 932 square feet
Second Floor: 780 square feet
Total: 1,712 square feet
Bedrooms: 3
Bathrooms: 2½
Width: 50'-0" **Depth:** 38'-8"

MEMORIES . . .

This home's square frame, lap siding, decorative shutters and covered stoop invite recollections of a quaint house from a friendly small town in our past or a relative's traditional farm house we often visited.

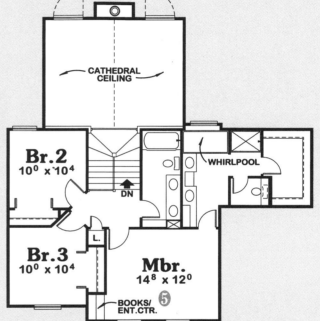

CATHEDRAL
CEILING

Br. 2
10⁰ x 10⁴

DN

WHIRLPOOL

Br. 3
10⁰ x 10⁴

L.

Mbr.
14⁸ x 12⁰

BOOKS/
ENT. CTR.

⑤

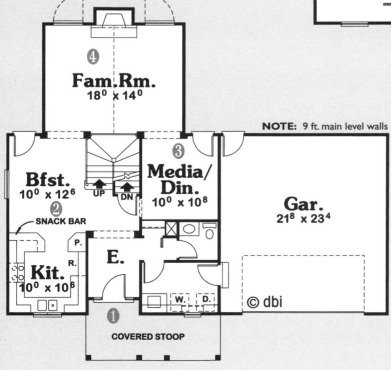

④

Fam. Rm.
18⁰ x 14⁰

NOTE: 9 ft. main level walls

Bfst.
10⁰ x 12⁶

UP   DN

③

**Media/
Din.**
10⁰ x 10⁸

Gar.
21⁸ x 23⁴

② SNACK BAR

P.

R.

Kit.
10⁰ x 10⁸

E.

W.   D.

© dbi

①

COVERED STOOP

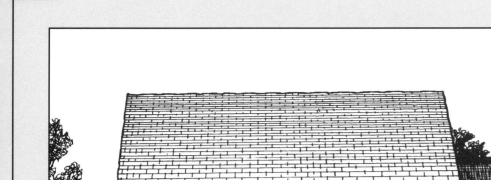

THE WAKEFIELD

❶ An arched opening and decorative half walls give the great room and dining room their character.

❷ A rear entry staircase in this home streamlines everyday traffic to the second floor.

❸ A built-in bench in the entry makes a quaint focal point and is helpful when removing shoes.

❹ The abundant space in the great room will be much appreciated when entertaining family, friends and guests.

❺ Two double—hung windows bring a cheerful atmosphere to the laundry room which features a soaking sink.

❻ The privacy of the master suite is enhanced by double doors and a location that is opposite two secondary bedrooms.

PLAN HPT040076

Type: Two-Story
First Floor: 1,067 square feet
Second Floor: 739 square feet
Total: 1,806 square feet
Bedrooms: 3
Bathrooms: 2½
Width: 55'-4" **Depth:** 32'-0"

MEMORIES . . .

The roomy great room in this home jogs memories of family reunions where aunts pinched your cheeks and told you how much you'd grown, uncles squeezed your biceps and challenged you to arm wrestle and cousins who started out as awkward strangers became long-lasting friends.

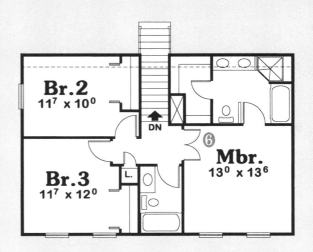

Br.2
11^7 x 10^0

DN

Br.3
11^7 x 12^0

L.

⑥

Mbr.
13^0 x 13^6

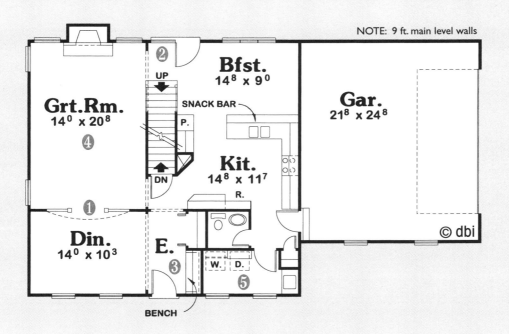

NOTE: 9 ft. main level walls

②

UP

Bfst.
14^8 x 9^0

Grt.Rm.
14^0 x 20^8

④

P.

SNACK BAR

Gar.
21^8 x 24^8

DN

Kit.
14^8 x 11^7

R.

①

Din.
14^0 x 10^3

E.

③

W. D.

⑤

© dbi

BENCH

DESIGNERS' INK

THE CRESWELL

❶ A stunning garden room with abundant windows and twin skylights will be a great place to entertain and display greenery.

❷ The large walk-thru kitchen provides plenty of counter space and is near the charismatic dining room with French doors.

❸ A second-floor balcony secludes three secondary bedrooms and overlooks the large great room with fireplace.

❹ Unfinished storage space on the second floor provides room to expand the master suite.

❺ A rear entry staircase streamlines daily traffic to the second floor.

❻ A mud entry from the garage provides a built-in bench and is near a powder bath and laundry room.

PLAN HPT040077

Type: Two-Story
First Floor: 837 square feet
Second Floor: 977 square feet
Total: 1,814 square feet
Bedrooms: 4
Bathrooms: 2¹/₂
Width: 58'-4" **Depth:** 41'-4"

MEMORIES . . .

When you were young, you were capti-
vated by a bird building a nest, a squir-
rel leaping from one tree to the next, a
baby rabbit hiding in tall grass. This
lovely garden room will entice you to
relish nature's wonders again.

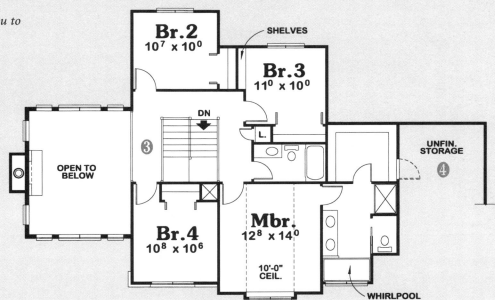

Br.2
10^7 x 10^0

SHELVES

Br.3
11^0 x 10^0

OPEN TO BELOW

DN

③

L.

UNFIN. STORAGE

④

Br.4
10^8 x 10^6

Mbr.
12^8 x 14^0

10'-0" CEIL.

WHIRLPOOL

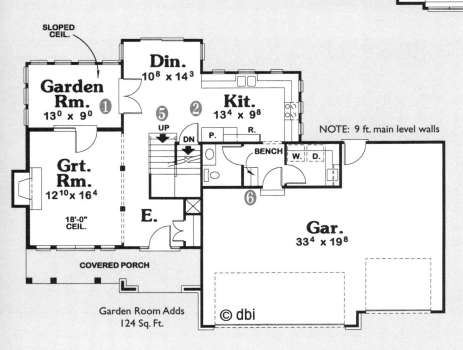

SLOPED CEIL.

Garden Rm.
13^0 x 9^0 ①

Din.
10^8 x 14^3

⑤ ② Kit.
13^4 x 9^8

UP

DN

P.

R.

NOTE: 9 ft. main level walls

Grt. Rm.
12^{10} x 16^4

18'-0" CEIL.

E.

BENCH

W. D.

⑥

Gar.
33^4 x 19^8

COVERED PORCH

Garden Room Adds
124 Sq. Ft.

© dbi

THE LANCASTER

❶ The two-story entry has a large coat closet with a plant shelf above.

❷ A spacious great room features large windows and a lovely fireplace.

❸ A boxed window over the sink is a pleasing detail in the island kitchen.

❹ Washing clothes is simpler with a main floor laundry.

❺ The front bedroom has a large arched window and a sloped ceiling.

❻ His and her walk-in closets are an added bonus in the master bedroom, as well as a double vanity and whirlpool in the bath.

PLAN HPT040078

Type: Two-Story
First Floor: 919 square feet
Second Floor: 927 square feet
Total: 1,846 square feet
Bedrooms: 4
Bathrooms: 2½
Width: 44'-0" **Depth:** 40'-0"

MEMORIES . . .

Why do porches evoke such warmth? They
remind us of a grandfather whittling a
piece of wood, a father playing the harmon-
ica, children grooming the dog, neighbors
"shooting the breeze." This roomy porch
will provide a perfect place to get away
from the hustle and bustle.

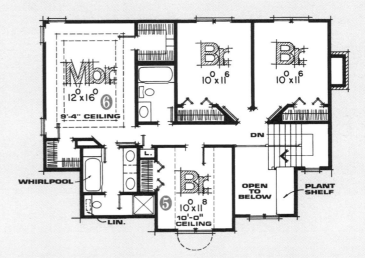

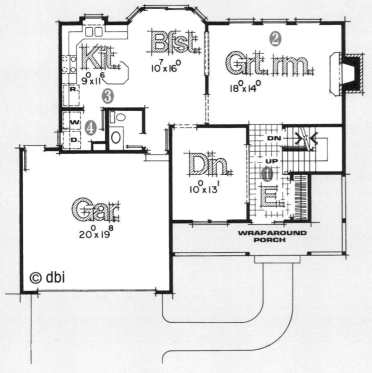

DESIGNERS'INK

THE COHASSET

1 This captivating design features beautiful windows set off with traditional, simplified trim.

2 Upon walking in, the front room has a variety of options including a parlor or, with its close vicinity to the kitchen, a dining room.

3 Bookshelves and a fireplace add a comfortable atmosphere to the family room.

4 Extra storage space in the garage welcomes shelves or a work bench.

5 Ample space is offered in the secondary bedrooms, both of which have a walk-in closet.

6 Unfinished storage above the garage would make a great addition to the master suite's closet, especially for seasonal storage.

PLAN HPT040079

Type: Two-Story
First Floor: 920 square feet
Second Floor: 973 square feet
Total: 1,893 square feet
Bedrooms: 3
Bathrooms: 2½
Width: 41'-4" **Depth:** 44'-0"

MEMORIES . . .

One of the quirks of growing up is look-
ing back fondly on chores you once dis-
dained. Like the time you spent in the
kitchen helping Mom with the dishes. As
you worked, you filled her in on all the
details of your day at school. This open
kitchen seems to beckon that kind of
teamwork—and sharing.

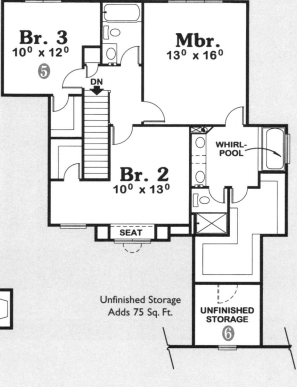

Unfinished Storage
Adds 75 Sq. Ft.

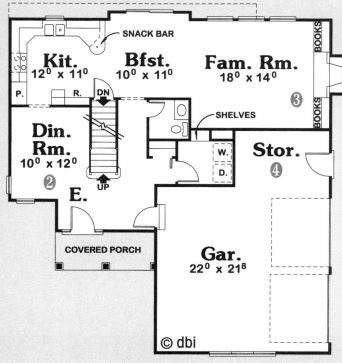

NOTE: 9 ft. main level walls

© dbi

THE BRANFORD

① Soldier coursing charms the windows of this home, which will make a good candidate for a narrow-lot situation.

② In its traditional role, the living room in this home welcomes guests as they walk in the door.

③ The hearth room offers a bookcase and shares a see-thru fireplace with the living room.

④ A computer area at the top of the stairway is perfect for homework or finishing up office work.

⑤ The unfinished bonus room on the second floor is a great place to expand into a studio.

⑥ Nine-foot main level walls bring a sense of spaciousness to all rooms on the first floor.

PLAN HPT040080

Type: Two-Story
First Floor: 1,002 square feet
Second Floor: 926 square feet
Total: 1,928 square feet
Bedrooms: 3
Bathrooms: 2½
Width: 46'-0" **Depth:** 51'-0"

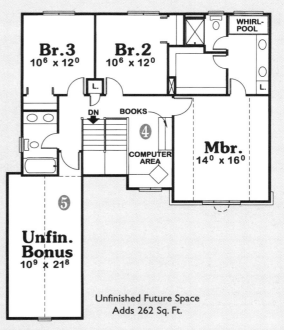

Br.3
10⁶ x 12⁰

Br.2
10⁶ x 12⁰

WHIRL-POOL

L.

DN

BOOKS

④

L.

Mbr.
14⁰ x 16⁰

COMPUTER AREA

⑤

Unfin. Bonus
10⁹ x 21⁸

Unfinished Future Space
Adds 262 Sq. Ft.

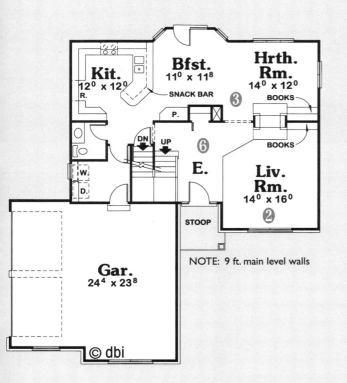

Kit.
12⁰ x 12⁰
R.

Bfst.
11⁰ x 11⁸

SNACK BAR

Hrth. Rm.
14⁰ x 12⁰

③

BOOKS

P.

BOOKS

DN   UP

⑥

E.

Liv. Rm.
14⁰ x 16⁰

②

W

D

STOOP

NOTE: 9 ft. main level walls

Gar.
24⁴ x 23⁸

© dbi

MEMORIES . . .

As a child, some of your favorite times were family game night when the whole family gathered to play Chutes and Ladders, Yahtzee, Crazy Eights or Monopoly. What better place to relive those wonderful memories than this cozy hearth room?

THE DARIUS

❶ A view of the living room, with elegant columns, sets the mood for the rest of the home.

❷ The dining room, when paired with the living room, shares space for formal occasions.

❸ The kitchen and breakfast area open spaciously to the family room, and are ideal for family celebrations.

❹ Upstairs, the master bedroom offers many options with its unfinished bonus space, great for storage or a private office.

❺ The master bath is lavish with its corner whirlpool tub and novel sloped ceiling.

PLAN HPT040081

Type: Two-Story
First Floor: 1,091 square feet
Second Floor: 847 square feet
Total: 1,938 square feet
Bedrooms: 3
Bathrooms: 2½
Width: 49'-0" **Depth:** 40'-0"

NOTE: 9 ft. main level walls

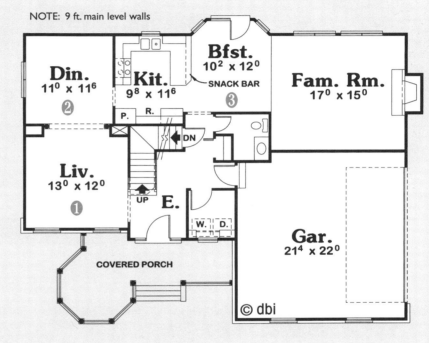

Din.
11⁰ x 11⁶
②

Kit.
9⁸ x 11⁶

Bfst.
10² x 12⁰

SNACK BAR

Fam. Rm.
17⁰ x 15⁰

P. R.

③

DN

Liv.
13⁰ x 12⁰
①

UP

E.

W. D.

Gar.
21⁴ x 22⁰

© dbi

COVERED PORCH

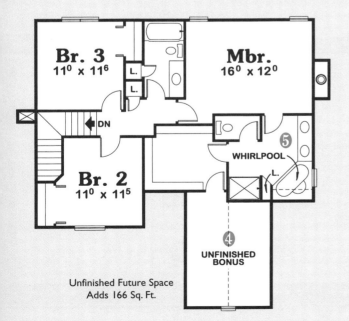

Br. 3
11⁰ x 11⁶

L.
L.

DN

Mbr.
16⁰ x 12⁰

⑤

WHIRLPOOL

L.

Br. 2
11⁰ x 11⁵

④

UNFINISHED
BONUS

Unfinished Future Space
Adds 166 Sq. Ft.

MEMORIES . . .

This picturesque gazebo stirs remembrances of ice cream socials, barbershop quartets, checkers games with Grandpa, moonlit serenades, romantic candlelit dinners and picture-perfect summer days.

THE SUMMERFIELD

① With a front porch that runs the width of this home, the elevation is stunning.

② Off the formal front entry you will find a coat closet, powder room and den with see-thru fireplace.

③ French doors in the dining area lead to a three-season porch which is also viewed from the living room.

④ An angled ceiling and a lovely arched window adorn the master bedroom which features a two-sink vanity, whirlpool tub and a large walk-in closet.

⑤ Just off the master suite, an unfinished storage area could also be converted to an office or hobby room.

⑥ Another large unfinished storage area is available off the hall near the laundry room.

PLAN HTP040082

Type: Two-Story
First Floor: 1,015 square feet
Second Floor: 945 square feet
Total: 1,960 square feet
Bedrooms: 3
Bathrooms: 2½
Width: 59'-0" **Depth:** 39'-0"

MEMORIES . . .

A highlight of childhood was the annual birthday party. We dressed up, put on pointed hats, played Bingo and pin-the-tail on the donkey, ate fancy cake and ice cream and opened lots of presents. Every year we wanted to invite a few more guests. This combined dining and hearth room area is big enough to do just that.

NOTE: 9 ft. main level walls

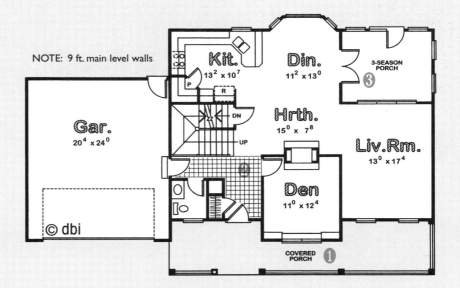

Kit.
$13^2 \times 10^7$

Din.
$11^2 \times 13^0$

3-SEASON PORCH ③

Gar.
$20^4 \times 24^0$

Hrth.
$15^0 \times 7^8$

Liv.Rm.
$13^0 \times 17^4$

Den
$11^0 \times 12^4$

© dbi

COVERED PORCH ①

Unfinished Storage Rooms
Add 402 Sq. Ft.

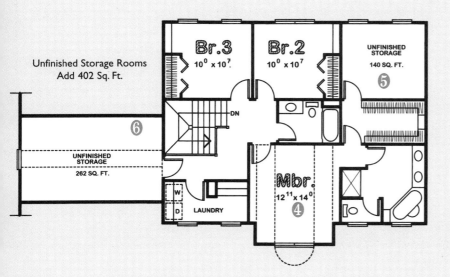

Br.3
$10^0 \times 10^7$

Br.2
$10^0 \times 10^7$

UNFINISHED STORAGE
140 SQ. FT. ⑤

DN

⑥

UNFINISHED STORAGE
262 SQ. FT.

W
D
LAUNDRY

Mbr.
$12^{11} \times 14^0$
④

THE LINDEN

①Handsome bookcases frame the fireplace and a large boxed window adds interest in the spacious family room.

②Double doors off the entry give the cozy family room privacy.

③The open breakfast/kitchen area provides a door to the back yard, built-in desk, work island, lazy Susan and easy access to the walk-in laundry.

④A window seat and special ceiling details accent the master bedroom which features separate entries into the walk-in closet and master bath.

⑤In the roomy master bath, two lavs, a linen closet, shower and whirlpool tub supply convenience and comfort.

⑥Upstairs, the hall bath is compartmented, allowing maximum usage for today's busy families.

PLAN HTP040083

Type: Two-Story
First Floor: 1,082 square feet
Second Floor: 1,021 square feet
Total: 2,103 square feet
Bedrooms: 4
Bathrooms: 2½
Width: 50'-0" **Depth:** 40'-0"

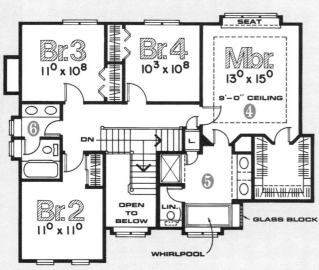

Br. 3
11⁰ x 10⁸

Br. 4
10³ x 10⁸

Mbr.
13⁰ x 15⁰

9'–0" CEILING

SEAT

④

⑥

DN

L.

⑤

Br. 2
11⁰ x 11⁰

OPEN
TO
BELOW

LIN.

GLASS BLOCK

WHIRLPOOL

MEMORIES . . .

Growing up, your mother was your greatest cheerleader. She kept a huge box filled with childish drawings and scrawled essays, plastered the refrigerator with your paintings and put your lopsided clay pot on her dresser. A window seat in the master bedroom would make a great place for a mom to dream her own dreams.

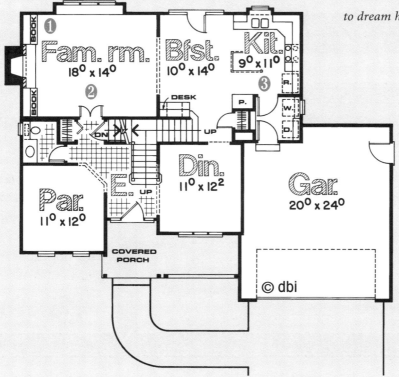

❶

BOOK

Fam. rm.
18⁰ x 14⁰

❷

BOOK

Bfst.
10⁰ x 14⁰

DESK

Kit.
9⁰ x 11⁰

❸

R.

P.

W.

D.

UP

DN

Par.
11⁰ x 12⁰

UP

Din.
11⁰ x 12²

Gar.
20⁰ x 24⁰

© dbi

COVERED
PORCH

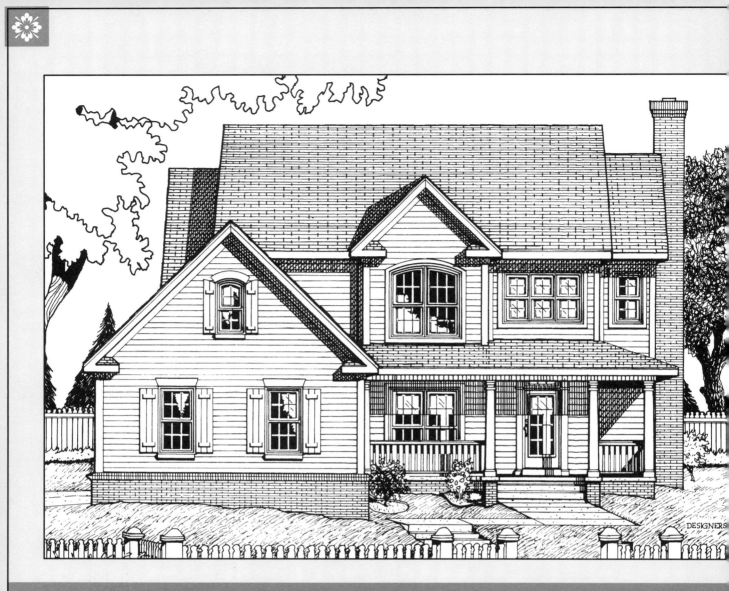

THE RIDGEVILLE

❶ The wrapping front porch sets off striking, second story windows.

❷ A pair of coat closets and a U-shaped stairway bring visual impact to the entry.

❸ The spacious great room easily accommodates guests and is within steps of the dining room when entertaining.

❹ An island counter and sink with window above benefit the kitchen, which is near an enclosed laundry room.

❺ Bedrooms 2 and 3 offer extra storage space in their walk-in closets and share a compartmented bath with bedroom 4.

❻ An indented entry brings a sense of presence to the master suite, which features a full bath with whirlpool tub and double vanity.

PLAN HPT040084

Type: Two-Story
First Floor: 1,006 square feet
Second Floor: 1,099 square feet
Total: 2,105 square feet
Bedrooms: 4
Bathrooms: 3½
Width: 47'-0" **Depth:** 43'-0"

MEMORIES . . .

The covered porch on this home conjures images of a simpler time. A timid young man waiting at the door holding a bouquet of flowers. The same young man walking his date to the door, making small talk and wondering whether he should kiss her good night.

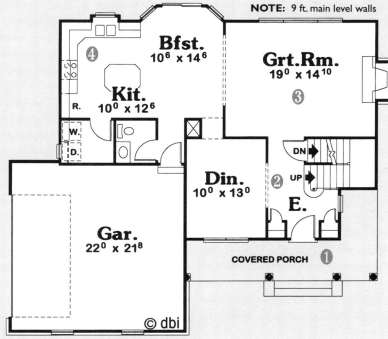

NOTE: 9 ft. main level walls

Bfst.
10^6 x 14^6

Grt.Rm.
19^0 x 14^{10}

③

④

Kit.
10^0 x 12^6

R.

W.

D.

DN

UP

Din.
10^0 x 13^0

②

E.

Gar.
22^0 x 21^8

COVERED PORCH   **①**

© dbi

WHIRLPOOL

⑤

Br.2
10^6 x 10^0

Mbr.
15^0 x 14^{10}

⑤

L.

⑥

Br.3
10^0 x 12^3

DN

Br.4
10^0 x 11^8

Loft
9^4 x 7^4

THE CALDERA

① Through the front covered porch is a lovely entry that views the staircase and offers a large coat closet with old-fashioned double doors.

② The great room is warmed by a fireplace and opens to the dining room for ease when entertaining.

③ The kitchen has ample counter space and a snack bar that serves the breakfast area.

④ The master suite is spacious, with its giant walk-in closet that further opens to more storage space.

⑤ Three secondary bedrooms, one with a handy built-in desk, share a full hall bath.

⑥ A pocket door leads to the laundry room providing a soaking sink.

PLAN HPT040085

Type: Two-Story
First Floor: 1,008 square feet
Second Floor: 1,136 square feet
Total: 2,144 square feet
Bedrooms: 4
Bathrooms: 2½
Width: 43'-8" **Depth:** 46'-0"

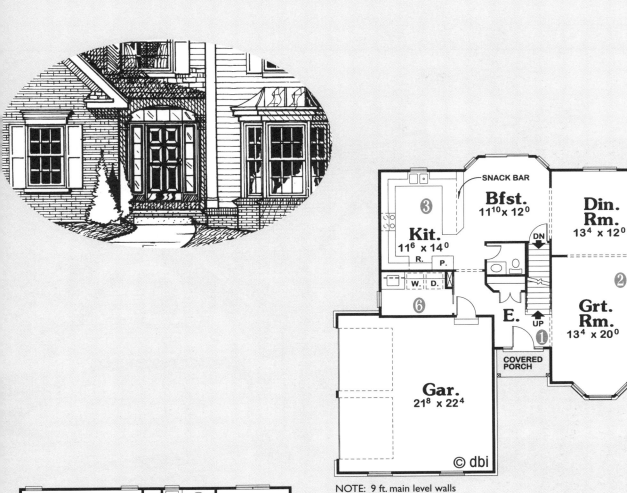

Bfst.
11^{10} x 12^0

SNACK BAR

Kit.
11^6 x 14^0

③

R.

P.

W. D.

⑥

Din. Rm.
13^4 x 12^0

DN

Grt. Rm.
13^4 x 20^0

②

E.

UP

①

COVERED PORCH

Gar.
21^8 x 22^4

© dbi

NOTE: 9 ft. main level walls

Mbr.
16^7 x 14^0

WHIRLPOOL

DESK

L.

L.

DN

⑤

Br. 3
10^0 x 14^3

Br. 4
11^4 x 10^4

Br. 2
13^4 x 11^0

④

Stor.
9^4 x 8^4

Unfinished Storage
Adds 88 Sq. Ft.

MEMORIES . . .

The perfect spot for a Christmas tree, the large bayed area in the great room draws recollections of trees of the past. Some too big for the amount of decorations on hand, some with drooping branches and some with bare spots. But with a little tinsel and a lot of lights, they all were gorgeous in the end.

THE CRAWFORD

① Spacious two-story entry surveys formal dining room with hutch space.

② A see-thru fireplace and built-in entertainment center highlight the great room.

③ Combined kitchen/breakfast/hearth areas feature gazebo dining, wrapping counters and numerous amenities.

④ Bedroom 3 features half-round transom and volume ceiling.

⑤ Bedroom 4 includes a built-in desk and an appealing boxed window.

⑥ In the master bedroom, a vaulted ceiling adds dramatic impact. In the master bath, a compartmented bath, his and her vanities and a whirlpool tub add convenience and comfort.

PLAN HPT040086

Type: Two-Story
First Floor: 1,150 square feet
Second Floor: 1,120 square feet
Total: 2,270 square feet
Bedrooms: 4
Bathrooms: 2½
Width: 46'-0" **Depth:** 48'-0"

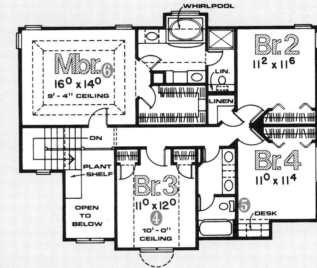

MEMORIES . . .

Remember begging your mom to teach you to bake a pie or make chocolate chip cookies? (You never seemed interested in learning how to cook vegetables.) Now that you're grown, the novelty of cooking may have worn off. But this open kitchen, complete with work island, will help you make the best of it.

WHIRLPOOL

Mbr. ⑥
16⁰ x 14⁰
9'- 4" CEILING

Br. 2
11² x 11⁶

LIN.

LINEN

Br. 4
11⁰ x 11⁴

DN

PLANT
SHELF

OPEN
TO
BELOW

Br. 3
11⁰ x 12⁰
④
10'- 0"
CEILING

⑤

DESK

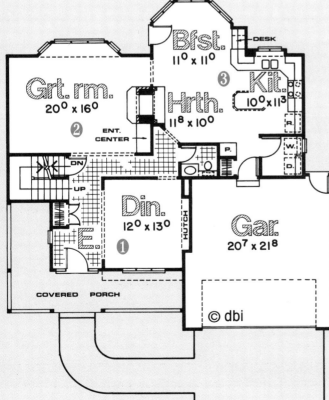

Bfst.
11⁰ x 11⁰

DESK

Grt. rm.
20⁰ x 16⁰

③

Kit.
10⁰ x 11³

②

ENT.
CENTER

Hrth.
11⁸ x 10⁰

R.

P.

DN

W.

UP

D.

Din.
12⁰ x 13⁰

HUTCH

Gar.
20⁷ x 21⁸

①

© dbi

COVERED   PORCH

THE AINSLEY

1 Plant shelves and stylish arches add beauty to the entry.

2 A spacious kitchen accommodates an island counter and large pantry, and is open to the bayed breakfast area and great room.

3 The T-shaped stairway facilitates traffic to the second floor.

4 A built-in dresser leaves room for more furniture in the master bedroom.

5 Reminiscent of an antique buffet, yet modernized for convenience, a servery near the dining room cuts down on trips to the kitchen.

6 The oversized laundry room has ample space to set up an ironing board.

PLAN HPT040087

Type: Two-Story
First Floor: 1,214 square feet
Second Floor: 1,118 square feet
Total: 2,332 square feet
Bedrooms: 4
Bathrooms: 2½
Width: 54'-0" **Depth:** 43'-4"

MEMORIES . . .

Hair—whatever ours was like, it was never right. Guys wished Dad would loosen up and let them wear it as long as their friends. Girls ironed it if it was too curly and permed it if it was too straight. These dual vanities in the upstairs baths will make taming hair simpler.

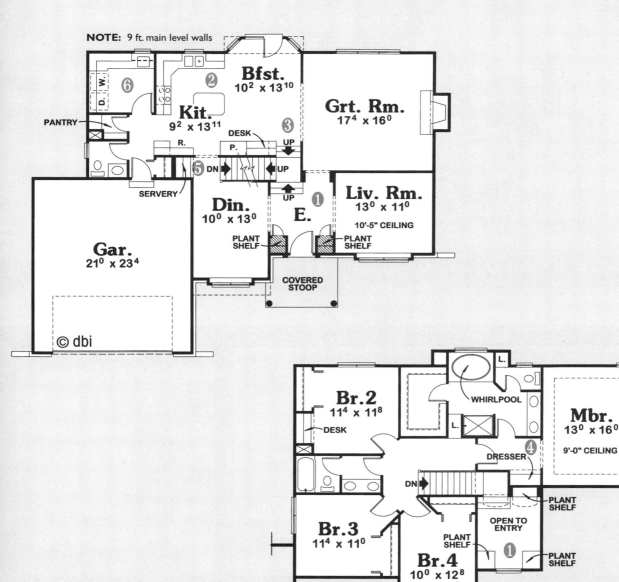

NOTE: 9 ft. main level walls

Bfst.
10^2 x 13^{10}

Grt. Rm.
17^4 x 16^0

Kit.
9^2 x 13^{11}

PANTRY

DESK

UP

UP

Liv. Rm.
13^0 x 11^0

10'-5" CEILING

DESK

P.

R.

DN

SERVERY

Din.
10^0 x 13^0

E.

PLANT SHELF

PLANT SHELF

Gar.
21^0 x 23^4

© dbi

UP

COVERED STOOP

Br.2
11^4 x 11^8

WHIRLPOOL

L.

L.

Mbr.
13^0 x 16^0

9'-0" CEILING

DESK

DRESSER

DN

PLANT SHELF

Br.3
11^4 x 11^0

OPEN TO ENTRY

PLANT SHELF

Br.4
10^0 x 12^8

PLANT SHELF

PLANT SHELF

THE KELLERTON

1 Formal rooms flank the foyer of this home and offer additional seating when hosting holiday gatherings.

2 An island cooktop is within steps of the sun-filled sink area in this convenient kitchen.

3 His and her walk-in closets are provided in the master suite.

4 Bedrooms 2 and 4 feature built-in desks which will be handy for homework and studying.

5 Across from a window in the laundry room is a soaking sink and counter space.

6 A deep storage nook in the garage offers adequate space for lawn and garden equipment.

PLAN HPT040088

Type: Two-Story
First Floor: 1,168 square feet
Second Floor: 1,165 square feet
Total: 2,333 square feet
Bedrooms: 4
Bathrooms: 2½
Width: 57'-4" **Depth:** 39'-8"

Memories . . .

The open floor plan in this home is bound to bring back images of the open house your parents threw to celebrate your high school graduation. There were balloons and streamers and people everywhere!

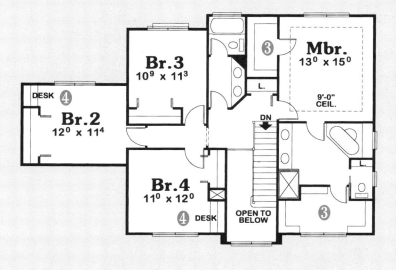

Br.3
10⁹ x 11³

③

Mbr.
13⁰ x 15⁰

9'-0"
CEIL.

DESK **④**

Br.2
12⁰ x 11⁴

L.

DN

Br.4
11⁰ x 12⁰

④ DESK

OPEN TO
BELOW

③

NOTE: 9 ft. main level walls

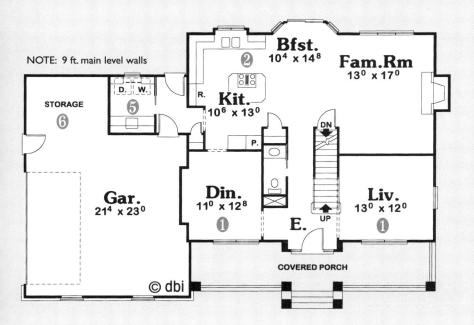

Bfst.
10⁴ x 14⁸

②

Fam.Rm
13⁰ x 17⁰

STORAGE
⑥

D. W.
⑤

R.

Kit.
10⁶ x 13⁰

P.

DN

Gar.
21⁴ x 23⁰

Din.
11⁰ x 12⁸

①

E.

UP

Liv.
13⁰ x 12⁰

①

© dbi

COVERED PORCH

THE GERARD

1️⃣ The elevation's understated styling is enhanced by the use of a variety of timeless architectural elements, such as its double-hung windows and shutters.

2️⃣ A wet bar in the family room is convenient when entertaining formally or informally.

3️⃣ The living and dining rooms will comfortably entertain guests and make beautiful places to show off antiques.

4️⃣ Bedroom 2 with its own private bath, makes the perfect guest bedroom or in-law suite.

5️⃣ Unfinished storage offers the potential for expansion.

6️⃣ At 50 feet in width, the Gerard helps solve a narrow lot situation.

PLAN HPT040089

Type: Two-Story
First Floor: 1,199 square feet
Second Floor: 1,150 square feet
Total: 2,349 square feet
Bedrooms: 4
Bathrooms: 3½
Width: 50'-0" **Depth:** 44'-0"

MEMORIES . . .

This formal living room reminds one of the parlor that was only used on Sundays when relatives came to visit. It was where the men gathered before dinner to discuss politics, crop prices and the merits of different automobiles—and where they nodded off after dinner.

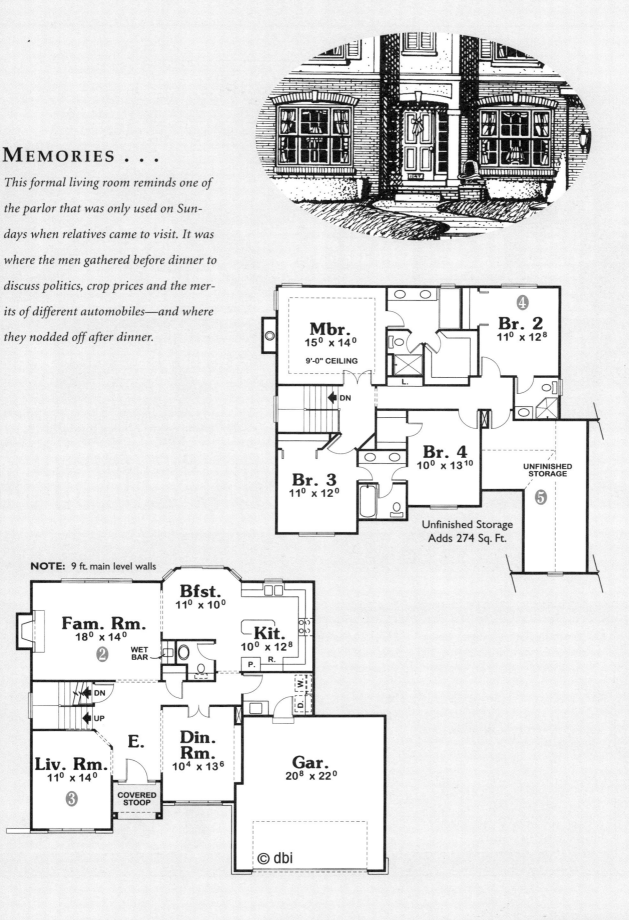

Mbr.
15^0 x 14^0

9'-0" CEILING

Br. 2
11^0 x 12^8

④

DN

L.

Br. 4
10^0 x 13^{10}

UNFINISHED STORAGE

⑤

Br. 3
11^0 x 12^0

Unfinished Storage
Adds 274 Sq. Ft.

NOTE: 9 ft. main level walls

Bfst.
11^0 x 10^0

Fam. Rm.
18^0 x 14^0

②

WET BAR

Kit.
10^0 x 12^8

P.   R.

DN

UP

D.   W.

Liv. Rm.
11^0 x 14^0

③

E.

Din. Rm.
10^4 x 13^6

Gar.
20^8 x 22^0

COVERED STOOP

© dbi

THE ALLISTON

❶ Complemented by brick pedestals and trim, the front porch is ideally suited to relaxing.

❷ A window brightens the U-shaped stairway that leads to a second floor landing overlooking the entry.

❸ Bayed windows in the great room, along with a warm fireplace, were designed to offer visual interest and to create an atmosphere for entertaining formally.

❹ An island cooktop is centrally located between the pantry, refrigerator and sink.

❺ A large linen cabinet, double vanity and whirlpool tub offer all of the necessities in the master bath.

❻ The laundry room offers the benefit of a hanging closet.

PLAN HPT040090

Type: Two-Story
First Floor: 1,256 square feet
Second Floor: 1,108 square feet
Total: 2,364 square feet
Bedrooms: 4
Bathrooms: 2½
Width: 46'-0" **Depth:** 48'-0"

MEMORIES . . .

The wealth of windows on the main floor of this home stimulates memories of sunny mornings when Mother went from room to room opening the blinds singing "Oh, let the sun shine in..." —and you followed pounding on the drum she'd made out of an empty Quaker Oats container.

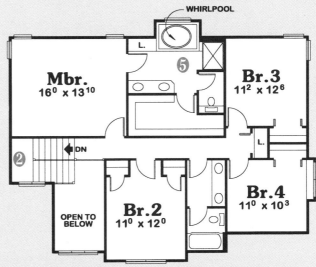

WHIRLPOOL

Mbr.
16⁰ x 13¹⁰

Br.3
11² x 12⁶

L.

⑤

② DN

L.

Br.2
11⁰ x 12⁰

Br.4
11⁰ x 10³

OPEN TO BELOW

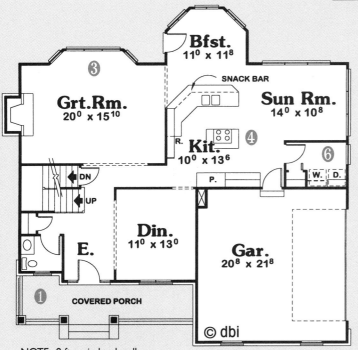

Bfst.
11⁰ x 11⁸

SNACK BAR

Grt.Rm.
20⁰ x 15¹⁰

Sun Rm.
14⁰ x 10⁸

R.

Kit.
10⁰ x 13⁶

④

⑥

W. D.

DN

UP

P.

Din.
11⁰ x 13⁰

Gar.
20⁸ x 21⁸

E.

① **COVERED PORCH**

© dbi

NOTE: 9 ft. main level walls

THE PATAGONIA

❶ French doors can be added to the bayed study to expand the family room.

❷ A built-in serving cabinet is strategically placed between the dining room and kitchen.

❸ A roll-a-way butcher block island is functional for the kitchen, but can easily be stored until needed.

❹ A rear covered porch is accessible from the breakfast area and is a great place to relax after a meal.

❺ The laundry room is conveniently located near the second floor bedrooms.

❻ Unfinished storage above the garage is beneficial for keeping seasonal items.

PLAN HPT040091

Type: Two-Story
First Floor: 1,162 square feet
Second Floor: 1,255 square feet
Total: 2,417 square feet
Bedrooms: 4
Bathrooms: 2½
Width: 58'-0" **Depth:** 42'-8"

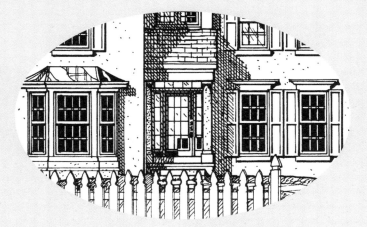

Second Floor

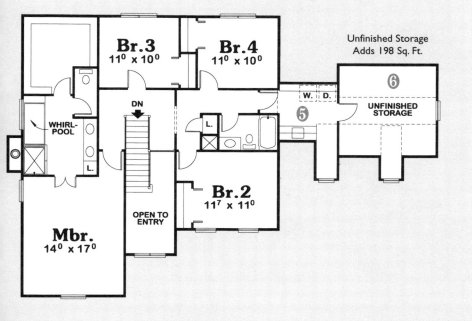

Br. 3
$11^0 \times 10^0$

Br. 4
$11^0 \times 10^0$

Unfinished Storage
Adds 198 Sq. Ft.

WHIRL-POOL

DN

W. D.

⑥

⑤

UNFINISHED STORAGE

OPEN TO ENTRY

Br. 2
$11^7 \times 11^0$

Mbr.
$14^0 \times 17^0$

First Floor

MEMORIES . . .

The layout of this home conjures images of Christmases past—tiptoeing down the long staircase during the night to see if Santa had arrived yet; racing back down those stairs early in the morning to peek into overstuffed stockings hanging over the fireplace.

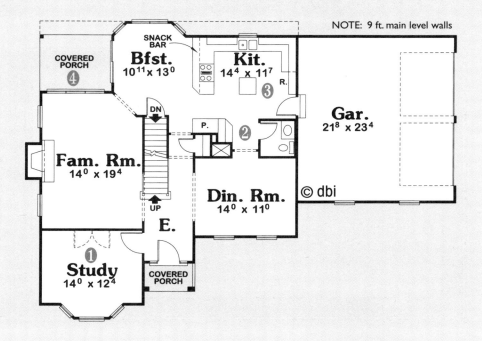

NOTE: 9 ft. main level walls

COVERED PORCH
④

SNACK BAR

Bfst.
$10^{11} \times 13^0$

Kit.
$14^4 \times 11^7$

R.

③

DN

P.

②

Gar.
$21^8 \times 23^4$

Fam. Rm.
$14^0 \times 19^4$

UP

E.

Din. Rm.
$14^0 \times 11^0$

© dbi

①

Study
$14^0 \times 12^4$

COVERED PORCH

THE NORWOOD

1 A cantilevered bayed window, wing wall and all-brick facade portray this home's hospitality.

2 A butler's pantry adjoins the kitchen and dining room, simplifying entertainment.

3 The spacious laundry room doubles as a mud room with a coat closet and soaking sink.

4 A second floor cedar closet provides seasonal clothes storage.

5 Special accommodations in the master suite include a built-in entertainment center and a walk-in closet with his and her sections.

6 Twin dormers add a view to the back in an exceptionally large bonus room.

PLAN HPT040092

Type: Two-Story
First Floor: 1,277 square feet
Second Floor: 1,198 square feet
Total: 2,475 square feet
Bedrooms: 3
Bathrooms: 2½
Width: 59'-4" **Depth:** 42'-8"

MEMORIES . . .

A built-in cedar closet prompts thoughts of Grandma's hope chest which contained your mother's christening dress, an ornate hand-made quilt, hand crocheted doilies and elaborately embroidered dresser scarves and pillow cases.

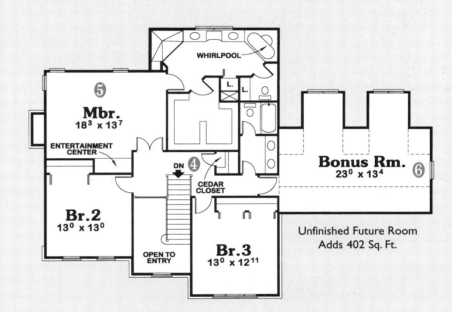

WHIRLPOOL

⑤

Mbr.
$18^3 \times 13^7$

ENTERTAINMENT CENTER

L. L.

DN **④**

CEDAR CLOSET

Br.2
$13^0 \times 13^0$

Bonus Rm.
$23^0 \times 13^4$ **⑥**

Unfinished Future Room
Adds 402 Sq. Ft.

OPEN TO ENTRY

Br.3
$13^0 \times 12^{11}$

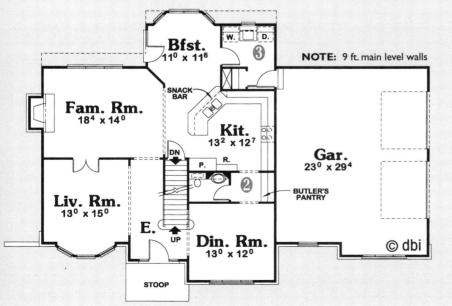

Bfst.
$11^0 \times 11^6$

W. D.

③

NOTE: 9 ft. main level walls

Fam. Rm.
$18^4 \times 14^0$

SNACK BAR

Kit.
$13^2 \times 12^7$

DN

P. R.

②

Gar.
$23^0 \times 29^4$

BUTLER'S PANTRY

Liv. Rm.
$13^0 \times 15^0$

E.

UP

Din. Rm.
$13^0 \times 12^0$

© dbi

STOOP

THE LARAMIE

1. Tucking a third stall beneath the front gable helps balance the look of this home's 3-car garage.

2. With a vaulted ceiling and triple window, the study could also be used as a formal dining room.

3. An open living room, kitchen and dining room allow easy mingling when entertaining.

4. A main floor guest suite is ideally located for privacy.

5. Flex space on the second floor could be used as a play room or fifth bedroom.

6. A walk-in closet, double vanity and vaulted ceiling are features in the master suite.

PLAN HPT040093

Type: Two-Story
First Floor: 1,323 square feet
Second Floor: 1,174 square feet
Total: 2,497 square feet
Bedrooms: 4
Bathrooms: 3
Width: 50'-0" **Depth:** 46'-0"

BEDROOM 2
12'6" X 11'6"

AC

MASTER
BEDROOM
12'6" X 17'

⑥

OPEN TO BELOW

⑤

DN

PLAY ROOM
12'6" X 14'6"

OPTIONAL
BEDROOM 5

BEDROOM 3
10'8" X 13'6"

OPEN
TO BELOW

ATTIC

AC

MEMORIES . . .

After church, we dashed to our rooms to change into comfortable clothes. Then we gathered in the living room and divided up the Sunday paper. Dad took the sports, Mom took the ads and the kids split the comics. There's plenty of room for everyone to spread newspaper pages out in this spacious living room.

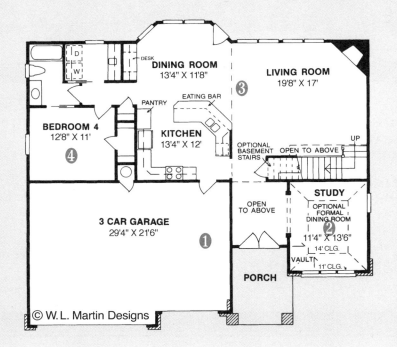

D
W

DESK

DINING ROOM
13'4" X 11'8"

LIVING ROOM
19'8" X 17'

③

PANTRY

EATING BAR

BEDROOM 4
12'8" X 11'

④

KITCHEN
13'4" X 12'

OPTIONAL
BASEMENT
STAIRS

OPEN TO ABOVE

UP

STUDY
OPTIONAL
FORMAL
DINING ROOM
11'4" X 13'6"
14' CLG.

②

VAULT
11' CLG.

3 CAR GARAGE
29'4" X 21'6"

①

OPEN
TO ABOVE

PORCH

© W.L. Martin Designs

THE LAVEEN

1 This Victorian-inspired design is enhanced with finials and scalloped shingles.

2 A deep alcove in the dining room will accommodate a cherished antique hutch.

3 French doors enclose the living room or expand it into the family room.

4 The island kitchen is accommodated by a large pantry and is brightened by the breakfast area.

5 All second floor bedrooms offer large walk-in closets.

6 The second floor corridor overlooks the two-story entry with a large plant shelf.

PLAN HPT040094

Type: Two-Story
First Floor: 1,122 square feet
Second Floor: 1,409 square feet
Total: 2,531 square feet
Bedrooms: 4
Bathrooms: 2½
Width: 57'-4" **Depth:** 33'-0"

Memories . . .

Remember when your bedroom was your own private sanctuary? A place to carry on phone conversations away from little sister's big ears. A place to hang posters of your favorite rock star or the car you planned to own someday. Having a room as big as bedroom 2 would have been a dream.

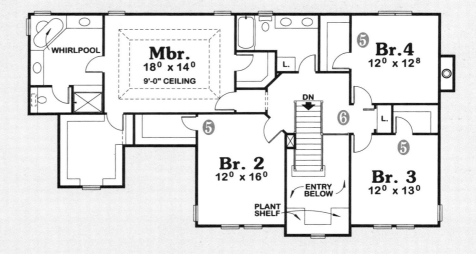

WHIRLPOOL

Mbr.
18^0 x 14^0

9'-0" CEILING

⑤ **Br. 4**
12^0 x 12^8

L.

DN

⑥

L.

⑤

Br. 2
12^0 x 16^0

ENTRY BELOW

⑤ **Br. 3**
12^0 x 13^0

PLANT SHELF

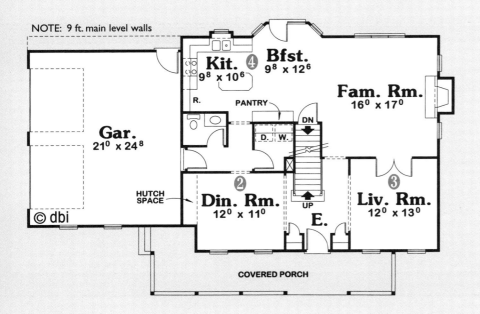

NOTE: 9 ft. main level walls

Kit.
9^8 x 10^6 ④

Bfst.
9^8 x 12^6

R.

PANTRY

DN

D. | W.

Fam. Rm.
16^0 x 17^0

Gar.
21^0 x 24^8

© dbi

HUTCH SPACE

② **Din. Rm.**
12^0 x 11^0

UP

E.

③ **Liv. Rm.**
12^0 x 13^0

COVERED PORCH

THE KARLYNDA

① Designed to appeal to the country-at-heart, this home welcomes guests with its deep front porch and nostalgic shutters.

② A large area for a hutch in the dining room will accommodate an antique.

③ The kitchen and breakfast area feature a walk-in pantry, island counter and bayed windows.

④ A large plant shelf, corner whirlpool tub and large walk-in closet with iron-a-way comprise a luxurious master suite.

⑤ A clothes chute is convenient to the secondary bedrooms within the main second-floor bath.

⑥ Extra storage in the garage allows for a work bench or sports equipment.

PLAN HPT040095

Type: Two-Story
First Floor: 1,266 square feet
Second Floor: 1,292 square feet
Total: 2,558 square feet
Bedrooms: 4
Bathrooms: 2½
Width: 54'-0" **Depth:** 44'-0"

MEMORIES . . .

With ample room for a workbench, this garage prompts memories of Grandpa skillfully mending a broken toy, tying fishing flies, building shelves for Grandma's knickknacks or tinkering with the toaster that went haywire.

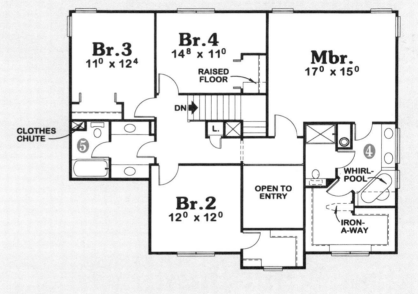

Br.3
11⁰ x 12⁴

Br.4
14⁸ x 11⁰

RAISED FLOOR

Mbr.
17⁰ x 15⁰

DN

CLOTHES CHUTE

L.

⑤

④

WHIRL-POOL

Br.2
12⁰ x 12⁰

OPEN TO ENTRY

IRON-A-WAY

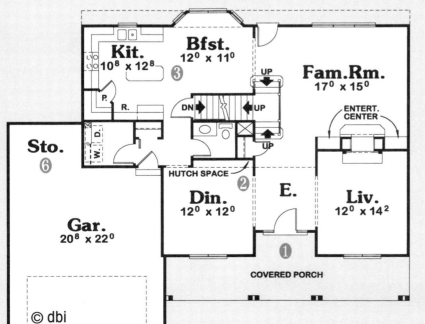

Kit.
10⁸ x 12⁸

Bfst.
12⁰ x 11⁰

③

UP

Fam.Rm.
17⁰ x 15⁰

P.

R.

DN

UP

ENTERT. CENTER

Sto.
⑥

W. D.

UP

HUTCH SPACE

②

Din.
12⁰ x 12⁰

E.

Liv.
12⁰ x 14²

Gar.
20⁸ x 22⁰

①

COVERED PORCH

© dbi

THE NEWBERRY

❶ French doors provide extra privacy between the living room and dining room.

❷ An island kitchen features snack bar, pantry and lazy Susan.

❸ A sunroom adjoins the breakfast area with a convenient built-in desk.

❹ Multiple furniture arrangements are possible in this sunken family room with beamed ceiling and fireplace in the back.

❺ French doors lead to a spacious master bath, with a dramatic bayed window over the corner whirlpool tub.

❻ Secondary bedrooms share a compartmented bath with two vanities.

PLAN HPT040096

Type: Two-Story
First Floor: 1,322 square feet
Second Floor: 1,272 square feet
Total: 2,594 square feet
Bedrooms: 4
Bathrooms: 2¹/₂
Width: 56'-0" **Depth:** 48'-0"

MEMORIES . . .

When we were little, our favorite toys were usually our biggest. A rocking horse, a child size refrigerator, stove and table set, a playhouse or a cardboard fort. Finding a place to keep them was usually a problem. This optional play room would have been great!

Optional Play Area
Adds 80 Sq. Ft.

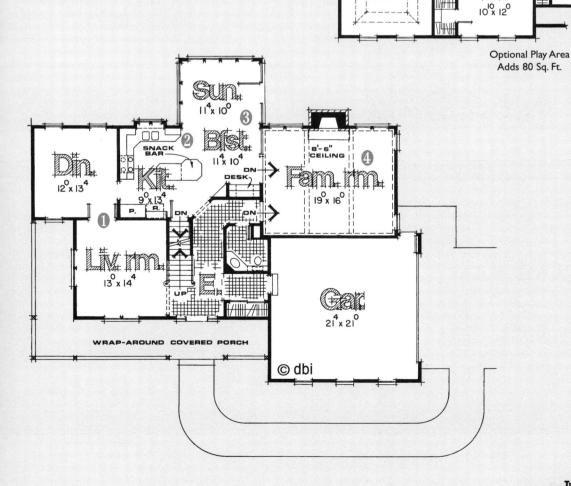

© dbi

WRAP-AROUND COVERED PORCH

THE CALABRETTA

❶ Classic lines define the statuesque look of this home.

❷ In keeping with traditional early American design, the formal rooms flank the entry and provide views to the front.

❸ An angled snack bar in the kitchen serves the breakfast area that is bathed in natural light.

❹ Bedroom 2 is the perfect guest suite with its own ¾ bath.

❺ His and her walk-in closets and an extravagant bayed whirlpool tub under a cathedral ceiling set the tone in the indulging master suite.

❻ A large bonus room has the potential to meet the preferences of many buyers.

PLAN HPT040097

Type: Two-Story
First Floor: 1,333 square feet
Second Floor: 1,280 square feet
Total: 2,613 square feet
Bedrooms: 4
Bathrooms: 3½
Width: 58'-0" **Depth:** 44'-4"

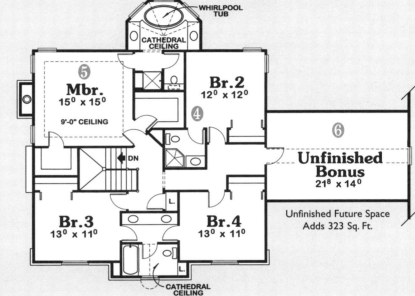

MEMORIES . . .

If you're old enough, you probably grew up with home movies. You lined up in your Sunday best and were admonished to move for the camera. So you waved and made "horns" behind your brother's head. This unfinished bonus room would make a great theater for watching home movies—or videos.

WHIRLPOOL TUB

CATHEDRAL CEILING

⑤ **Mbr.** 15⁰ x 15⁰
9'-0" CEILING

Br.2 12⁰ x 12⁰

④

⑥ **Unfinished Bonus** 21⁸ x 14⁰

Unfinished Future Space Adds 323 Sq. Ft.

DN

L.

Br.3 13⁰ x 11⁰

Br.4 13⁰ x 11⁰

L.

CATHEDRAL CEILING

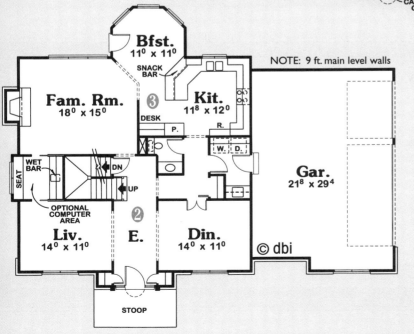

Bfst. 11⁰ x 11⁰
SNACK BAR

NOTE: 9 ft. main level walls

Fam. Rm. 18⁰ x 15⁰

③ **Kit.** 11⁸ x 12⁰

DESK

P.

R.

W. D.

WET BAR

SEAT

DN

OPTIONAL COMPUTER AREA

UP

②

Gar. 21⁸ x 29⁴

Liv. 14⁰ x 11⁰

E.

Din. 14⁰ x 11⁰

© dbi

STOOP

THE PEBBLE BROOK

❶ Views of the formal dining room and open staircase add elegance to the front entry.

❷ French doors provide privacy in the study.

❸ A corner fireplace allows for a built-in entertainment center in an optimal location.

❹ Angled walls in the breakfast area and bedroom 3 add interest to the rooms.

❺ Unfinished storage over the garage is accessed from the hall on the second floor.

❻ A special computer alcove on the second level offers the perfect spot to play games, work on homework or finish up some details from the office.

PLAN HPT040098

Type: Two-Story
First Floor: 1,285 square feet
Second Floor: 1,345 square feet
Total: 2,630 square feet
Bedrooms: 4
Bathrooms: 2½
Width: 59'-1½" **Depth:** 51'-9"

Memories . . .

When we were young, we put bedtime off as long as we could. First, a snack. Then a story and a shadow puppet performance. And finally, our prayers and one last drink of water. Now grown-up, we often can't wait to get to bed. After a long, busy day, this master suite would be a great place to unwind.

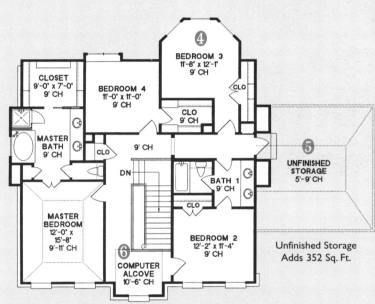

CLOSET
9'-0" x 7'-0"
9' CH

BEDROOM 4
11'-0" x 11'-0"
9' CH

BEDROOM 3
11'-8" x 12'-1"
9' CH

CLO

CLO
9' CH

MASTER
BATH
9' CH

CLO

9' CH

DN

BATH 1
9' CH

⑤

UNFINISHED
STORAGE
5'-9' CH

MASTER
BEDROOM
12'-0" x
15'-8"
9'-11' CH

CLO

BEDROOM 2
12'-2" x 11'-4"
9' CH

Unfinished Storage
Adds 352 Sq. Ft.

⑥

COMPUTER
ALCOVE
10'-6" CH

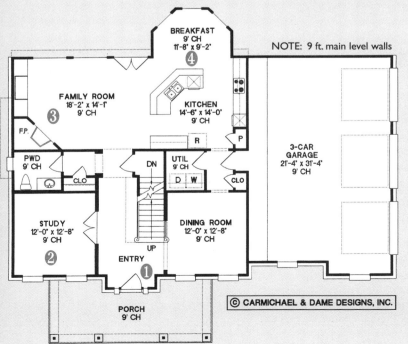

BREAKFAST
9' CH
11'-8" x 9'-2"
④

NOTE: 9 ft. main level walls

FAMILY ROOM
18'-2" x 14'-1"
9' CH
③

KITCHEN
14'-6" x 14'-0"
9' CH

F.P.

PWD
9' CH

CLO

R

P

UTIL
9' CH

DN

D W

CLO

3-CAR
GARAGE
21'-4" x 31'-4"
9' CH

STUDY
12'-0" x 12'-8"
9' CH

②

ENTRY
①

DINING ROOM
12'-0" x 12'-8"
9' CH

UP

© CARMICHAEL & DAME DESIGNS, INC.

PORCH
9' CH

THE SUTTER

1. A subdued exterior hints at this home's colonial roots.

2. The two-story entry is enhanced with an open, second-floor balcony.

3. A barrel-vault ceiling leads to the great room which offers a comforting see-thru fireplace.

4. The kitchen, with an island counter and double oven, is conveniently located near the dining room and bayed breakfast area.

5. Highlighting the master suite area are a boxed ceiling, oval whirlpool tub and French doors.

6. Bedroom 4 can be an optional sitting room with access from the master suite.

PLAN HPT040099

Type: Two-Story
First Floor: 1,357 square feet
Second Floor: 1,285 square feet
Total: 2,642 square feet
Bedrooms: 4
Bathrooms: 2½
Width: 56'-0" **Depth:** 48'-0"

MEMORIES . . .

As you look through old family pictures, you notice how many were taken around the Christmas tree, beside a new car or in front of the house. Wouldn't this make a distinguished-looking home to pose in front of?

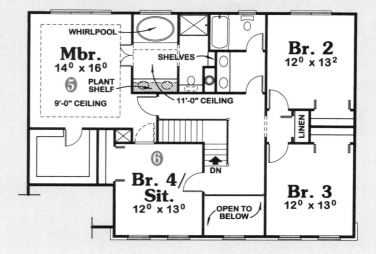

WHIRLPOOL

Mbr.
14^0 x 16^0

SHELVES

Br. 2
12^0 x 13^2

⑤ PLANT SHELF

9'-0" CEILING

11'-0" CEILING

LINEN

⑥

DN

Br. 4/ Sit.
12^0 x 13^0

OPEN TO BELOW

Br. 3
12^0 x 13^0

NOTE: 9 ft. main level walls

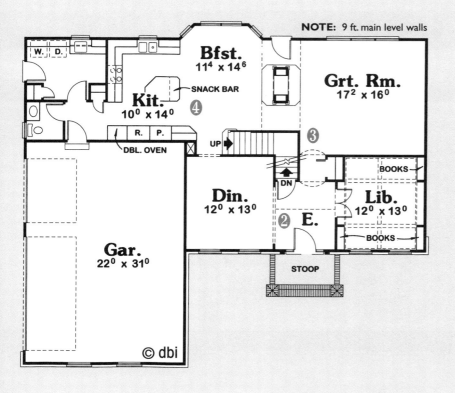

W. D.

Bfst.
11^4 x 14^6

SNACK BAR

Grt. Rm.
17^2 x 16^0

Kit.
10^0 x 14^0 ④

R. P.

DBL. OVEN

UP

③

BOOKS

Din.
12^0 x 13^0

DN

② **E.**

Lib.
12^0 x 13^0

BOOKS

Gar.
22^0 x 31^0

STOOP

© dbi

THE WOODVINE MANOR

❶ An open entry provides pleasing views into formal living and dining rooms.

❷ In the family room, windows on the front and back walls, a fireplace and a beamed cathedral ceiling add drama.

❸ A quiet covered porch on the back of the home is accessed from the breakfast area.

❹ A spacious island kitchen, with ample cabinets and counter tops, opens to a large, sunny breakfast area.

❺ The master bedroom enjoys bayed windows and an angled ceiling.

❻ A sunken location provides a bit of drama for the master bath with two walk-in closets, his and her vanities and a whirlpool tub.

PLAN HPT040100

Type: Two-Story
First Floor: 1,400 square feet
Second Floor: 1,315 square feet
Total: 2,715 square feet
Bedrooms: 4
Bathrooms: 2½
Width: 75'-1½" **Depth:** 38'-0"

Memories . . .

Over the years you've probably worn your share of amusing attire: footed pajamas and stocking caps with ear flaps... paisley and polka dot shirts... hip-hugger bell bottoms and platform shoes. With four walk-in closets, you might be tempted to hang onto a few old clothes—just for laughs.

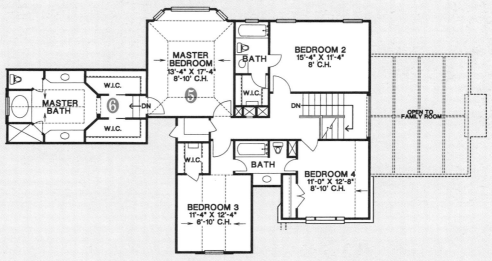

MASTER BEDROOM
13'-4" X 17'-4"
8'-10" C.H.

BATH

BEDROOM 2
15'-4" X 11'-4"
8' C.H.

W.I.C.

W.I.C.

MASTER BATH

W.I.C.

⑥

DN

⑤

DN

OPEN TO FAMILY ROOM

W.I.C.

BATH

BEDROOM 4
11'-0" X 12'-8"
8'-10" C.H.

BEDROOM 3
11'-4" X 12'-4"
6'-10" C.H.

NOTE: 9 ft. main level walls

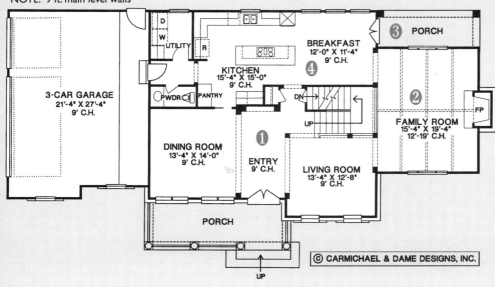

3-CAR GARAGE
21'-4" X 27'-4"
9' C.H.

D
W
UTILITY
R

PWDR
PANTRY

KITCHEN
15'-4" X 15'-0"
9' C.H.

BREAKFAST
12'-0" X 11'-4"
9' C.H.

③ PORCH

④

②

FAMILY ROOM
15'-4" X 19'-4"
12'-19' C.H.

FP

DINING ROOM
13'-4" X 14'-0"
9' C.H.

① ENTRY
9' C.H.

DN
UP

LIVING ROOM
13'-4" X 12'-8"
9' C.H.

PORCH

UP

© CARMICHAEL & DAME DESIGNS, INC.

THE ATTLEBORO

① While making a smart impression from the street, this home features a roofline that can easily be trussed.

② An optional guest bedroom on the main floor offers flexibility as family needs change.

③ A walk-in pantry in the island kitchen accommodates the needs of the whole family.

④ Nine-foot main level walls give a sense of spaciousness to first floor rooms.

⑤ Sturdy columns frame the dining room-sure to make special occasions even more memorable.

⑥ The whole family will be accommodated with three bedrooms and a master suite on the second level.

PLAN HPT040101

Type: Two-Story
First Floor: 1,582 square feet
Second Floor: 1,170 square feet
Total: 2,752 square feet
Bedrooms: 4
Bathrooms: 3½
Width: 53'-4" **Depth:** 54'-4"

MEMORIES . . .

Remember spending the night at a relative's home—camping out on their living room floor? It seemed you just got to sleep when your cousins pounced on top of you in the wee hours of the morning. Imagine how nice it would have been to stay in a secluded guest room—with a private bath.

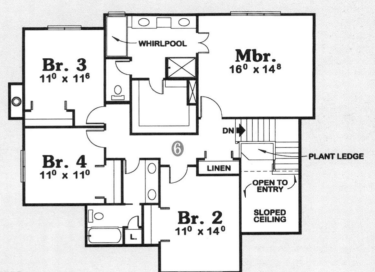

WHIRLPOOL

Br. 3
$11^0 \times 11^6$

Mbr.
$16^0 \times 14^8$

Br. 4
$11^0 \times 11^0$

DN

⑥

LINEN

PLANT LEDGE

OPEN TO ENTRY

Br. 2
$11^0 \times 14^0$

SLOPED CEILING

L.

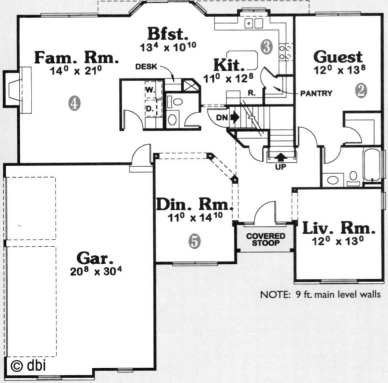

Fam. Rm.
$14^0 \times 21^0$

Bfst.
$13^4 \times 10^{10}$

③

Kit.
$11^0 \times 12^8$

Guest
$12^0 \times 13^8$

DESK

W.

D.

R.

PANTRY

②

④

DN

UP

Din. Rm.
$11^0 \times 14^{10}$

⑤

COVERED STOOP

Liv. Rm.
$12^0 \times 13^0$

Gar.
$20^8 \times 30^4$

© dbi

NOTE: 9 ft. main level walls

STUDY PRINT & FURNITURE LAYOUT GUIDE™

For many home buyers, visualizing the finished home is a challenge. Our **Study Print & Furniture Layout Guide**™ makes it easy. First, the Study Print provides views of all exterior elevations. Secondly, the Furniture Layout Guide provides a "Feel" for room sizes, with a 1/4" scale floor plan, over 100 reusable furniture pieces and helpful tips on space planning.

– Available for any Design Basics plan –

only $29.95

CUSTOMIZED PLAN CHANGES

PRICE SCHEDULE

2 X 6 EXTERIOR WALLS	$75
FROM STANDARD 2 X 4 TO 2 X 6 EXTERIOR WALLS	
EACH GARAGE ALTERATION	$325
• FRONT-ENTRY TO SIDE LOAD (OR VICE VERSA)	
• 2-CAR TO 3-CAR (OR VICE VERSA)	
• 2-CAR FRONT-ENTRY TO 3-CAR SIDE-LOAD (OR VICE VERSA)	
• 3-CAR FRONT-ENTRY TO 2-CAR SIDE-LOAD (OR VICE VERSA)	
WALK-OUT BASEMENT	$195
STRETCH CHANGES	$6 per lineal foot of cut
ADDITIONAL BRICK TO SIDES & REAR	$350
ADDITIONAL BRICK TO FRONT, SIDES AND REAR	$450
ALTERNATE PRELIMINARY ELEVATION	$195
9-FOOT MAIN LEVEL WALLS	starting at $195
SPECIFY WINDOW BRAND (WITHOUT OTHER CHANGES - $150)	$95
POURED CONCRETE FOUNDATION ONLY WITH OTHER CHANGES (WITHOUT OTHER CHANGES - $150)	$25
ADDING ONE COURSE (8") TO THE FOUNDATION HEIGHT ONLY WITH OTHER CHANGES (WITHOUT OTHER CHANGES - $150)	$25

NOTE

- All plan changes come to you on erasable, reproducible vellums.
- An unchanged set of original vellums is available for only $50 along with your plan changes.
- Design Basics changes are not made to the artist's renderings, electrical, sections or cabinets.
- Prices are subject to change.

CUSTOMIZE
any home plan

As a part of our commitment to help you achieve the "perfect" home, we offer an extensive variety of plan changes for any Design Basics plan. For those whose decision to purchase a home plan is contingent upon the feasibility of a plan change, our Customer Support Specialists will, in most cases, be able to provide a FREE price quote for the changes.

Three Foundations
For Every Plan

All Design Basics Home Plans come complete with a basement foundation. Now you can add a slab or crawl space foundation without paying for a custom change.

ONLY $75 EACH

AVAILABLE ON ALL DESIGN BASICS PLANS

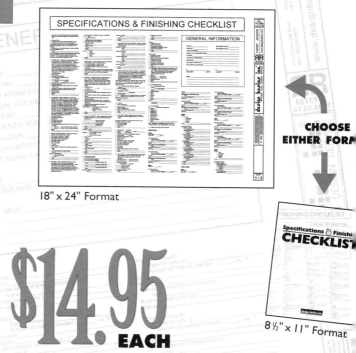

Specifications & Finishing
CHECKLIST™

With this handy **reference tool** you'll never forget the little things. Each decision you need to make during the construction of your home is outlined in an easy-to-follow format. Everything from the types of excavation to the brand and style of doorknobs.

No builder or consumer should be without the Specifications & Finishing Checklist™ from Design Basics.

18" × 24" Format

CHOOSE EITHER FORM

8½" × 11" Format

$14.95 EACH

DESIGN BASICS' HOME PLAN LIBRARY

1.

2.

3.

1) Impressions of Home™ Homes Designed with the Look You Want – 100 designs from 1339' to 4139'. $4.95

2) Impressions of Home™ Homes Designed for the Way You Live – 100 designs from 1191' to 4228'. $4.95

3) Impressions of Home™ Homes & Places for Real People – 100 designs from 1341' to 4139'. $4.95

4) Heartland Home Plans™
120 plan ideas designed for everyday practicality. Warm, unpretentious elevations easily adapt to individual lifestyles. From 1212' to 2631'. $8.95

5) Reflections of an American Home™ Vol. III
50 photographed home plans with warm remembrances of home and beautiful interior presentations. From 1341' to 3775'. $4.95

6) Photographed Portraits of an American Home™
100 of our finest designs, beautifully photographed and tastefully presented among charming photo album memories of "home". A must for any sales center's coffee table. $14.95

7) Gold Seal™ Home Plan Book Set – 442 of today's most sought-after one-story, 1 ¹/₂ story and 2-story home plan ideas. All 5 books for $50.00 or $10.00 each

- Homes of Distinction – 86 plans under 1800'
- Homes of Sophistication – 106 plans, 1800'-2199'
- Homes of Elegance – 107 plans, 2200'-2599'
- Homes of Prominence – 75 plans, 2600'-2999'
- Homes of Grandeur – 68 plans, 3000'-4000'

8) Timeless Legacy™, A Collection of Fine Home Designs by Carmichael & Dame – 52 breathtaking luxury home designs from 3300' to 4500'. Includes artful rear views of each home. $15.00

9) The Homes of Carmichael & Dame™ Vol. II
60 elegant designs from simple to sublime. From 1751' to 4228'. $9.95

10) *Seasons of Life™
Designs for Reaping the Rewards of Autumn
100 home plans specially tailored to today's empty-nester. From 1212' to 3904'. $4.95

11) *Seasons of Life™
Designs for Living Summer's Journey – 100 designs for the move-up buyer. From 1605' to 3775'. $4.95

12) *Seasons of Life™
Designs for Spring's New Beginnings – 100 home plans for first-time buyers. Presentations unique to this lifestyle. From 1125' to 2537'. $4.95

13) W.L. Martin Home Designs™
53 beautiful home plans offering outstanding livability. From 1262' to 3914'. $9.95

14) The Narrow Home Plan™ Collection
258 one-story, 1 ¹/₂ story and 2-story home plans that are from 26 to 50 feet wide. Many can be joined together to create customized duplex plans. $14.95

15) Nostalgia Home Plans Collection™
A New Approach to Time-Honored Design
70 designs showcasing enchanting details and unique "special places." From 1339' to 3480'. $9.95

16) Nostalgia Home Plans Collection™ Vol. II
A New Approach to Time-Honored Design
70 designs bringing back the essence of homes of the past. $9.95

17) Gold Seal Favorites™ – 100 best selling plans from the famous Gold Seal™ Collection, including 25 duplex designs. $6.95

18) Easy Living One-Story Designs™
155 one-story home designs from the Gold Seal™, Heartland Home Plans™ and Timeless Legacy™ collections, together in one plan book. $7.95

*Order the complete Seasons of Life™ set (all three books) for only $9.00

18.

17.

16.

15.

14.

13.

12.

11.

10.

9.

8.

7.

6.

5.

4.

COPYRIGHT
Cans & Cannots

These days, it seems almost everybody has a question about what can or cannot be done with copyrighted home plans. At Design Basics, we know US copyright law can sometimes get complex and confusing, but here are a few of the basic points of the law you'll want to remember.

Once you've purchased a plan from us and have received a Design Basics construction license,

You Can ...

■ Construct the plan as originally designed, or change it to meet your specific needs.

■ Build it as many times as you wish *without* additional reuse fees.

■ Make duplicate blueprint copies as needed for construction.

You Cannot ...

■ Build our plans without a Design Basics construction license.

■ Copy *any* part of our original designs to create another design of your own.

■ Claim copyright on changes you make to our plans.

■ Give a plan to someone else for construction purposes.

■ Sell the plan.

PROTECT YOUR RIGHTS

to build, modify and reproduce our home plans with a Design Basics construction license.

The above points are provided as general guidelines only. Additional information is provided with each home plan purchase, or is available upon request at (800) 947-7526.

CONSTRUCTION LICENS

as original purchaser of plan number

is hereby granted a non-transferable, non-exclusive license to build the home depi ed in this plan and is given the right to reproduce this plan only as required for suc construction. No re-use fee is required if the original purchaser builds this home mor than once. Permission is also given to make modifications to this plan, but no permis sion is given to claim copyright on the original or any derivative works of this plan. No other rights are granted and any further distribution is strictly prohibited.

Signed _____
Date _____
License Number _____

RETAIN IN YOUR FILES
FOR FUTURE REFERENCE

Valid when the
official Gold Seal™
is embossed above.

11112 John Galt Boulevard   Omaha, Nebraska 68137
Toll Free 800-947-PLAN
402-331-9223   FAX 402-331-5507

design basics inc.
HOME PLAN DESIGN SERVICE

PRICE SCHEDULE & PLAN INDEX

DESIGN BASICS' PLAN PRICE SCHEDULE
FOR ONE SET OF MASTER VELLUMS

Tiers	1-set Study Package	4-set Building Package	8-set Building Package	1-set Reproducible Sepias	Home Customizer® Package
A1	$400	$440	$500	$600	$650
A2	$440	$480	$540	$660	$710
A3	$480	$520	$580	$720	$770
A4	$520	$560	$620	$780	$830
C1	$560	$600	$660	$840	$890
C2	$600	$640	$700	$900	$950
C3	$650	$690	$750	$950	$1000
C4	$700	$740	$800	$1000	$1050
L1	$750	$790	$850	$1050	$1100
L2	$800	$840	$900	$1100	$1150
L3	$900	$940	$1000	$1200	$1250
L4	$1000	$1040	$1100	$1300	$1350

www.designbasics.com

A Plan From Design Basics: What's In It For You?

Plans come to you on high-quality reproducible vellums and include the following:

1. Cover Page. Each Design Basics home plan features the rendered elevation and informative reference sections including: general notes and design criteria;* abbreviations; and symbols for your Design Basics' plan.

2. Elevations. Drafted at ¼" scale for the front and ⅛" scale for the rear and sides. All elevations are detailed and an aerial view of the roof is provided, showing all hips, valleys and ridges.

3. Foundations. Drafted at ¼" scale. Block foundations and basements are standard. We also show the HVAC equipment, structural information,* steel beam and pole locations and the direction and spacing of the floor system above.

4. Main Level Floor Plan. ¼" scale. Fully dimensioned from stud to stud for ease of framing. 2"x4" walls are standard. The detailed drawings include such things as structural header locations, framing layout and kitchen layout.

5. Second Level Floor Plan. ¼" scale. Dimensioned from stud to stud and drafted to the same degree of detail as the main level floor plan.*

6. Interior Elevations. Useful for the cabinet and bidding process, this page shows all kitchen and bathroom cabinets as well as any other cabinet elevations.

7. Electrical and Sections. Illustrated on a separate page for clarity, the electrical plan shows suggested electrical layout for the foundation, main and second level floor plans. Typical wall, cantilever, stair, brick and fireplace sections are provided to further explain construction of these areas.

All plan orders received prior to 2:00 p.m. CT will be processed, inspected and shipped out the same afternoon via 2nd business day air within the continental United States. All other product orders will be sent via UPS ground service. Full Technical Support is available for any plan ⬛chase from Design Basics. Our Technical Support Specialists provide unlimited technical s⬛port free of charge and answer questions regarding construction methods, framing techniq⬛and more. Please call 800-947-7526 for more information.

CONSTRUCTION LICENSE

When you purchase a Design Basics home plan, you receive a Construction License w⬛gives you certain rights in building the home depicted in that plan, including:

No Re-Use Fee. As the original purchaser of a Design Basics home plan, the Cons⬛tion License permits you to build the plan as many times as you like.

Local Modifications. The Construction License allows you to make modifications⬛your Design Basics plans. We offer a complete custom change service, or you may h⬛the desired changes done locally by a qualified draftsman, designer, architect or engine⬛

Running Blueprints. Your plans are sent to you on vellum paper that reproduces well⬛your blueprint machine. The Construction License authorizes you or your blueprint faci⬛at your direction, to make as many copies of the plan from the vellum masters as ⬛need for construction purposes.

*Our plans are drafted to meet average conditions and codes in the state of Nebraska, at the time they are designed. Because codes and requirements can change and may vary from jurisdiction to jurisdiction, Design Basics Inc. cannot warrant compliance with any specific code o⬛regulation. All Design Basics plans can be adapted to your local building codes and requirements. It is the responsibility of the purchaser and/or builder of each plan to see that the structure is built in strict compliance with all governing municipal codes (city, county, state and federa⬛

CALL 800-521-6797

Name _____

Address _____
(For UPS Delivery – Packages cannot be shipped to a P.O. Box.)

Above Address: ☐ business address ☐ residence address

☐ VISA **VISA**   ☐ **MasterCard** (MasterCard)

We appreciate it when you use VISA or MasterCard.

Credit Card:

☐ Check enclosed   ☐ AMEX   ☐ Discover

Signature _____

Company _____

Title _____

City _____ State _____ Zip _____

Phone ( ) _____ FAX ( ) _____

Expiration Date: ☐☐ / ☐☐

✔	HOME PLAN PRODUCTS	PLAN #	QTY.	PRICE	SHIPPING & HANDLING	TOTAL
☐	1 Complete Set of Master Reproducible/Modifiable Vellum Prints					$
☐	Add'l. Sets of Blueprints - $20.00					$
☐	Add'l. Sets of Mirror Reverse Blueprints - $20.00					$
☐	Materials & Estimator's Workbook - $50.00					$
☐	Study Print & Furniture Layout Guide - $29.95					$
☐	Custom Furniture Plans™ - $39.95					$
☐	Complete Plan Book Library – $150.00					$
BOOK NUMBER	BOOK NAME					
						$
						$

• CALL FOR • Shipping & Handling Charges

• No COD Orders • US Funds Only •
NO REFUNDS OR EXCHANGES, PLEASE

Subtotal	$	
TX Res. Add 6.25% Tax (on #9126-#9143-#9160 -#9162-#9170 only) NE Residents Add 6.5% Sales Tax	$	
Total	$	

PRICES SUBJECT TO CHANGE

To Order Call (800) 521-6797

These 100 time-honored designs, from 1,191 to 3,040 square feet, capture the nostalgia of homes lovingly linked to the past. What is it we find so deeply alluring about these homes of yesteryear? Is it the beauty of their intricately crafted details? Is it the memories they stir up that inevitably reminds us of the homes we grew up in?

It's all of these things and more. Design Basics' Nostalgia Home Plans was created to help you rediscover the homes of the past. Comfortably familiar, you'll find homes with time-honored detailing updated with today's floor plans and features. Each home highlights specific elements, offering further insight into the design that may help you choose a home that best suits your needs.

What you may feel is missing in the homes of today, you'll find in the Nostalgia Home Plans collection—designs to help you recreate the warmth and beauty of houses you can be proud to call home.

ISBN 1-881955-69-9

$14.95
($20.95 Canada)

HOME PLANNERS, LLC
Wholly owned by Hanley-Wood, LLC
3275 W. INA RD., SUITE 110, TUCSON, ARIZONA 85741

www.homeplanners.com

ISBN 1-881955-6

0 29129 95569 5

9 781881 955696